Winning Low-Limit Hold'em

Lee Jones

Other ConJelCo titles:

Books

Software

Winning Low-Limit Hold'em

Lee Jones

ConJelCo
Pittsburgh, Pennsylvania

Winning Low-Limit Hold'em
Copyright © 2005 by Lee Jones

Publisher's Cataloging-in-Publication Data

Jones, Lee

Winning Low-Limit Hold'em/Lee Jones.
xii, 276 p. : ill. ; 22 cm.

ISBN-13 978-1-886070-23-3
ISBN-10 1-886070-23-7
I. Title.

Library of Congress Control Number: 2005926438

Third Edition

7 9 8 6

This edition has been issued with two different covers. The content is the same regardless of the cover.

The "Bee" Ace of Spades is a registered trademark ® of the United States Playing Card Corporation and is used with their kind permission.

ConJelCo LLC
1460 Bennington Ave.
Pittsburgh, PA 15217-1139
[412] 621-6040
http://www.conjelco.com

For Barry Tanenbaum

Whose friendship is a daily blessing. There are few greater pleasures than arguing politics with Barry over a good pastrami sandwich.

Contents

Foreword

Thanks to the success of the World Poker Tour, Chris Money-maker's improbable World Series Win in 2003, and wall-to-wall poker coverage on ESPN, everyone wants to play Texas Hold'em.

Most of these new players have watched many more hours of televised poker than they've actually played themselves. They've seen pros like Gus Hansen, holding two over cards, push his opponent off a made hand by making massive, aggressive, seemingly insane bets. They think, "Hey, I can totally bluff like that," and before they know it they're at the casino, making their fifth trip to the cash machine in two hours.

I love people who play like this. In fact, if you're one of these people, I'd like to invite you out to Los Angeles to play with me. You can even sit to my left

. . . Unless you read and study this book. Because after you've spent a few hours with Lee Jones, you'll have a solid foundation in poker, and you won't make the mistakes that experienced players pounce on and use to break you. You will have a serious edge over the suckers, you'll throw away seemingly big hands when you're drawing nearly dead, you'll make the right (not always the obvious) play before and after the flop. You'll instinctively know what your odds really are of making that flush or straight, and if it's worth it to make the call or quietly fold. You will recognize the futility of stone-cold bluffing in limit games, and when you walk to the cashier with more chips than you had when you sat down, you can finally tip out a little bit, Mister Big Shot.

Some of you may be wondering, *"Why in the world are* you *writing this foreword? You're not even a pro!"*

The short answer to your question is: because I owe much of my success as a poker player to Lee Jones. *Winning Low-Limit Hold'em* is the book that transformed me from Biggest Fish In The World to the winning player I am today.

The longer answer is: I've played poker since high school — though I hesitate to refer to all those crazy dealer's choice games as real poker — so when the hold'em craze caught fire a few years ago, I played every chance I got . . . and everyone wanted me in their game, because I was a *bad* player. I over-valued marginal hands, I tried to bluff too often, and I even thought that I had to defend my blind in a 2-4 limit game when I held an unsuited 5-3. (If you don't read past this paragraph, let me do you a solid: Unless it's checked to you and you make a big hand on the flop, throw that trash away, all the time, no matter what. You're welcome.)

In an effort to improve my game, I invested hundreds of dollars in many no-limit poker books. I watched hours of World Poker Tour and Celebrity Poker Showdown. I read thousands of posts on Usenet. I dumped an embarrassing amount of money ~~playing~~ chasing online, and an equally embarrassing amount playing the 1-2 limit game at the Commerce Casino just outside Los Angeles. Let me tell you, if you can lose a lot of money playing 1-2 limit, you've got trouble.

About two years ago, I played in a no-limit hold'em tournament here in Los Angeles. I was way over my head, and I had no business even entering, but somehow I finished third, and I published a story about it called *Lying in Odessa* on my blog. It generated a lot of e-mail from readers who enjoyed the drama, and experienced poker players who laughed out loud at my lousy (but lucky) play. One experienced poker player who didn't mock me was Lee Jones, who enjoyed the story, but (correctly) thought my game needed a lot of work. He kindly offered me a copy of this book.

Never one to refuse the kindness of strangers, especially when it could potentially plug some gaping holes in my poker game, I gratefully accepted. The second edition of this book arrived in the mail a few days later, and I began to study.

I was only about thirty or so pages into it when I realized that I was not just a bad poker player . . . I was, in fact, one of the worst poker players in the world. I was . . . *a fish*. Spurred on by this horrifying revelation, I continued to study. The concepts and advice Lee lays out in this book were all so simple, so *obvious*, and so easy to immediately apply to my game, I couldn't understand why more people didn't use them. Of course, thousands of hands later I *do* know why: most of the people you're going to encounter in low-limit games are those people I described above. They've watched more poker on TV than they've actually played themselves, and they think that they can play low-limit games the same way the pros play no-limit games. And here is the key concept that Lee drilled into my head: *You can not play the same way in low-limit as you do in no-limit. If you do, you will consistently lose. A lot.* When I grokked that idea, I put Sklansky, Caro, Doyle, and TJ back on my bookshelf, and exclusively studied *Winning Low-Limit Hold'em*. "Someday," I thought, "I may be a no-limit player, but I need to learn how to walk before I can learn how to run."

My copy of this book is highlighted, underlined, dog-eared, and filled with post-its because this book — the very book you're holding right now — is the book that made all the difference for me. This book is the reason I can play a consistently profitable game. Before I read *Winning Low-Limit Hold'em*, I was just a guy who liked to play poker. After I read *Winning Low-Limit Hold'em*, I was a player. A Poker Player. A fish no more.

Because of the foundation (and bankroll) I built with Lee's help, I've been able to move up to the no-limit games, and I'm doing pretty well . . . but I never would have been able to do it without *Winning Low-Limit Hold'em.*

So I guess you could say that I got to write this foreword because you're probably very similar to Wil Wheaton version 2003: someone who likes to play poker, but wants to be a player. A Poker Player.

When you finish this book, and you have applied Lee's lessons to your game, I hope to see you in a cardroom . . . but you'll excuse me if I ask for a table change when you sit down next to me. I'd rather tangle with the suckers.

Namaste.

Wil Wheaton
Author, Actor and Future WSOP Champion
Pasadena, California
May, 2005

Foreword to the First Edition

To the list of the writers of great poker manuals — Sklansky and Malmuth, Brunson and Caro — we must now add the name of Lee Jones... For those on the nursery slopes of Hold'em, anxious to get it right before ascending to loftier levels — or those who've had their bankrolls burned at higher altitudes, and can swallow their pride long enough to start the long climb again — Lee has compiled the soundest advice I've ever read. I only hope I can summon the self-discipline to follow it myself. Play Lee Jones's user-friendly system, and you'll soon find yourself earning respect at any table in any card-room in the poker world.

And a whole bunch of bucks better off.

Anthony Holden — author of Big Deal
London, England
August 29, 1994

Foreword to the Second Edition

I'm delighted to be asked to write a foreword to the second edition of *Winning Low-Limit Hold'em*. Lee's book has changed the landscape of lower limit hold'em games over the past six years. If you don't know what's in this text, you're playing at a serious disadvantage to those who do. You have to pay for your poker lessons one way or another; *Winning Low-Limit Hold'em* is by far the cheaper tuition plan. Now, let's play hold'em.

Linda Johnson — former Publisher of Card Player
Las Vegas, NV
September 2000

Who Should Read This Book?

How often have you bought a book only to discover that it wasn't what you were after? Before you spend your money on this book, you should know if it's right for you. So, **Read this book if:**

- You have played some poker, but have never played hold'em and you'd like to give it a try. Maybe it just showed up in your Thursday night home game. Perhaps you've discovered that you can play poker on the Internet and want to give that a try. Maybe you're getting ready for a trip to Las Vegas and want to spend some time playing poker.[1] If you read this book through once, you'll be able to sit down and hold your own in just about any low-limit hold'em game.

- You are intrigued by the no-limit hold'em "sit-and-go" tournaments that are everywhere on the Internet.

- You've been playing hold'em for a month, or a year, or ten years, and you just can't beat it. You see the chips flying around the table, and once in a while you have to borrow a laundry bag to carry your winnings out, but sometimes you have to borrow the laundry bag to cover the upper half of your body. This book will help you find the problems in your game and correct them.

---

[1]This is worth considering. Unlike virtually every other game in Las Vegas casinos, you can have positive expected value (a monetary edge) at poker.

- You're holding your own in low-limit hold'em games. Occasionally, players will get up and leave when they see you sit down. Nevertheless, you think that you might be missing an extra bet or two every session. This book may give you some ideas on how to find that extra bet.

Don't read this book if:

- You've never played poker. If that's the case, then we strongly urge you to buy *Fundamentals of Poker* by Mason Malmuth and Lynne Loomis or *Poker for Dummies* by Richard Harroch and Lou Krieger. Read and start playing. Then come back here and start reading.

- You're routinely crushing the competition in a $30-$60 hold'em game in southern California. You don't need this book. However, we suggest that you frequently review *Hold'em Poker for Advanced Players* by David Sklansky and Mason Malmuth.

We hope you'll find this book worth reading.

♠   ♥   ♦   ♣

Introduction: Why a Book on Low-Limit Hold'em?

It's not like the world is clamoring for yet another hold'em book.[1] Furthermore, in our opinion, Sklansky and Malmuth have written the definitive text on how to play medium-limit hold'em. But there are differences in the low-limit games that justify a separate treatment.

What's the difference between low- and high-limit hold'em?

The concepts that you must understand to win at low-limit hold'em are the same as those for any hold'em game (or any poker game for that matter). However, many of the strategies and ideas presented in other texts are not applicable to low-limit games. This is not because those strategies are wrong, but because they are aimed at higher limit games and tougher opponents.

Why should the correct strategy for a low-limit game be different from a higher limit contest? After all, a $30-$60 game is just a $3-$6 game played with $10 chips. However, in general, the players in a $30-$60 game are stronger than those in a $3-$6 game. They know more about the game, odds, different plays, etc. Furthermore, the higher limit players are generally tighter. Fewer people will pay to see the flop in a $30-$60 game than will in a $3-$6 game. Therefore, there are some important strategic differences between the two games.

---

[1] This statement was written for the first edition of the book in 1994. A review of bookstore shelves suggests that it's no longer true.

Perhaps the biggest difference between low- and high-limit games can be summed up in a single word: mistakes. In a high-limit game, most players will be more experienced. They will make very few fundamental mistakes, and to beat them you will have to make the most of every small edge you get. On the other hand, in low-limit games, your opponents will generally make many fundamental errors. They will call when they should fold, check when they should bet, etc. Therefore, you don't need to capitalize on small mistakes. You can wait until you have a big advantage (either you have a very strong hand or your opponent has made a serious mistake) and then take maximum advantage of it. For that reason, your "variance" — the up and down swings in your bankroll — may be less than that of an expert player who plays in a tougher game.

I should note that since publishing the first edition of this book, I have seen many of the "low-limit" game conditions we describe in games as large as $15-$30 and $30-$60. Particularly in the California poker communities (and in some places on the Internet), many of the amateur players are quite well off, and some are very wealthy. Just as a rich businessman might choose to play blackjack for $100 per hand with no concept of basic strategy, some well-to-do amateur poker players play $20-$40 hold'em even though they know very little about the game. Of course, in the $20-$40 game, there will probably be a few players who are very good, but remember: you don't have a take a test to play higher limit games.

What will you learn from reading this book?

This book will teach you how to play correctly in those "No Fold'em" games. It will teach you which hands you can play, and which hands you can raise with. Perhaps most importantly, it will teach you when to fold. We'll cover various skills that you'll need to beat the low-limit hold'em game. In some places, we'll go a little deeper into the theory — why you're making a certain play rather than just what to do. You'll later learn that all of this knowledge makes an excellent foundation for moving into bigger and tougher games.

If you read and study this book carefully and then apply what you learn at the tables, you will be able to beat just about any low-limit hold'em game.

What is your goal?

This book will teach you to be a solid low-limit hold'em player. Like the best poker authors before us, we emphasize tight but aggressive play; this means you won't play many hands. You may find watching a lot of hands, as opposed to playing a lot of hands, boring. If your goal at the poker table is to have fun, do a lot of gambling, and catch an occasional miracle card, then you should not follow our recommendations. There is not a thing wrong with this approach to poker; however, you will not be a consistent winner. If that doesn't bother you, and you can afford the cost of your entertainment, we hope you enjoy yourself. On the other hand, if you get your satisfaction from winning the most money in your poker game, then you're on the right track by reading this book.

Note also that your opponents at the table will have different reasons for being at the table as well. Understanding their reasons for playing is a powerful tool to help you beat them.

What games does this book cover?

This book covers hold'em games from the online "micro-limits" ($.25-$.50 and smaller) up to $5-$10 or $6-$12. At the $10-$20 level and above, you will need some new skills, and you will see more solid players than in the lower limits. The example game in this text is a $3-$6 structured limit game (described in detail in "Hold'em Fundamentals" beginning on page 16).

In the first two editions of this book, I said that $3-$6 hold'em was the most commonly played game in U.S. public cardrooms. That may still be true, but the Internet has created an entire regime of "micro-limit" games, right down to $.05-$.10 (and smaller) hold'em. "No Fold'em Hold'em," as it's sometimes called, has mushroomed with the extraordinary growth of popularity in poker.

Poker popularity

I am almost at a loss for words to describe the growth of poker, and particularly hold'em, since the publication of the second edition of "WLLH" in 2000. I don't think anybody could have predicted the explosive growth of poker over the last four years; I surely didn't.[2] But in hindsight, there are three key factors: the Internet, poker on TV, and Chris Moneymaker.

The Internet

In the second edition, I hesitatingly spent three pages talking about poker and computers. But since the second edition was published a mere four years ago, the percentage of people in North America with access to the Internet has more than doubled, to 70% of the population. Now, the number of people playing poker on the Internet is undoubtedly greater than the number playing in "brick and mortar" cardrooms and casinos. Online poker has brought the game to hundreds of thousands of people who previously had no reasonable access to public poker. Consequently, this edition contains a long chapter devoted to online poker.

Television

When something shows up on television, it immediately has the American public's attention. A few tournaments (including the World Series of Poker) and TV producers tried to get poker onto the small screen — after all, poker is America's national card game. The resulting shows were, it must be said, dreadfully boring. In none of these shows could the viewers see the players' hole cards; watching poker that way is like watching paint dry.

Then in early 2002, the creators of the World Poker Tour TV show installed tiny "lipstick cameras" in a poker table to record the players' hole cards. Those card images were superimposed as screen graphics in postproduction, and all of a sudden, tele-

---

[2]I remember getting an email from my publisher in early 2004 telling me that the second edition of this book had briefly reached #95 on Amazon's bestseller list (out of a quarter-million titles). I laughed long and hard, absolutely sure that he was pulling my leg.

vised poker was riveting theater. The armchair player now knows who is bluffing and who has the goods. And, perhaps more importantly, we the audience know the right decision to make, even as we watch the player agonize over it. At this writing, World Poker Tour is the most popular show on the cable channel that carries it. Of course, other networks and shows have emulated the idea and poker is now ubiquitous on television, fueling a worldwide craze for the game.

Poker has been popular on American kitchen tables and in the back rooms of bars since the 19th century. But grocery store clerks and college-age women didn't ask you about the poker-related T-shirt you were wearing. Now it's the subject of major news magazine articles, and regular poker games are being announced in college dorms and on office bulletin boards. The top tournament players are treated like rock stars or movie celebrities. Television has brought poker into the mainstream.

Chris Moneymaker

It's rare that you can point to a single person as a driving force behind a nationwide (and worldwide) sports craze. But Chris Moneymaker is undoubtedly just such a force. Chris was an accountant for a restaurant in Nashville and played online poker for recreation. In the spring of 2003, he entered and won a $39 satellite no-limit hold'em tournament at PokerStars.com, an online poker site. That victory gave him an entry into a larger satellite tournament on PokerStars. He won that one as well, which gave him a seat in the $10,000 buy-in event at the 2003 World Series of Poker in Las Vegas. The "WSOP," as it's known, attracts the finest poker players from around the world. No serious odds maker would have given Chris any chance whatsoever — particularly if they had known that it was his first live poker tournament (as opposed to ones played on the Internet).

Chris stunned the odds makers and the whole world by outlasting over 800 other players at the WSOP and playing some very tough poker. He eventually beat Houston-based poker professional Sammy Farha in the heads-up final to win $2.5 million and the coveted championship bracelet.

This Cinderella story took Chris from the David Letterman show to the pages of the New York Times, and his easygoing demeanor and understated speech have captured fans around the world. They look at him and think, "He's a normal guy — just like me. I could do that too." Those "normal guys" (and gals) have turned up in droves at cardrooms, casino poker rooms, and online poker sites. Many of them hope to be the next Chris Moneymaker.[3]

About the third edition

I didn't plan to write a third edition of this book so soon, if ever. But all of the above has changed poker immeasurably, and essentially forced me to update the text to catch up with the times.

For one thing, the players are worse. The huge boom in poker popularity has created an unimaginable supply of poker novices; they will astonish you with their "generous" play. Also, because an online poker room can open another table for virtually no additional cost, they are happy to spread games much smaller than a "brick and mortar" operation could profitably manage. In earlier editions of this book, I said that $1-$2 hold'em games were dying out. That is no longer true. Not only are they thriving (online), but so are $.50-$1.00, $.25-$.50, and $.05-$.10 games. These "micro-limit" games give new meaning to the concept of "low-limit." This edition reflects that sea change in the player demographics.

I have had a long series of discussions with Barry Tanenbaum, whom I consider to be one of the clearest and most articulate thinkers in poker today. Those discussions have caused me to rethink some of my ideas about pre-flop and post-flop play, and those changes are reflected here. As an example, I've dramatically shortened the list of hands that are playable pre-flop, and recommended a "raise or fold" strategy when you're first into the pot in middle and late positions.

---

[3]Chris kept his job at the restaurant for a year after his WSOP victory. At this writing, he is doing consulting and endorsements in the poker industry, and, of course, playing serious tournament poker.

Another outcome of my discussions with Barry was the decision to stop using words such as "probably" and "usually." As Barry said, "Words like that do me no good unless you tell me what the exceptions are." So in many cases, I'll be telling you "zig," when in fact you should "zag" 5% of the time. Don't worry about it; the 5% zag cases aren't going to cost you significant profit, and it will dramatically simplify these lessons by ignoring that 5%. Furthermore, you will learn when to zag soon enough if you keep studying the game.

Finally, because the TV poker shows are built around tournaments, the popularity of poker tournaments (particularly no-limit hold'em events) has skyrocketed. Kitchen table games that had been built around "Follow the Queen" and "Baseball"[4] for years have suddenly turned into a series of no-limit hold'em tournaments. I thought that I needed to address this form of the game, but wanted to limit my focus. I have spent the last few years playing a lot of "sit-and-go" tournaments — one or two table tournaments that pay a percentage of the prize pool back to the last 3-4 players. These events are available all over the Internet, and are even showing up in live poker rooms now. And they can be incredibly profitable. So I have included a chapter on them.

Limit vs. no-limit; cash games vs. tournaments

Hold'em can be played in any of the common betting formats: limit, pot-limit, and no-limit. It can be played as a "cash" game, meaning that you are playing for cash (or chips that may be redeemed for cash). Or it can be played as a "tournament," meaning that the chips that you have can't be cashed out — you can only win money by finishing in the final few players in the event. Furthermore, any combination of betting format and cash/tournament is perfectly reasonable; in fact, all of these combinations are quite popular and actively played.

This book is almost exclusively about playing limit hold'em in a cash game. You can still learn something about playing a pot-

---

[4]These are bastardizations of seven-card stud. They will not be mentioned again in this text.

limit hold'em tournament from this book, but this book shouldn't be your only reference if you plan to be a pot-limit hold'em tournament specialist.

With that said, I have added, for the third edition, a chapter devoted to the other corner of the matrix: one-table no-limit hold'em tournaments (a "sit-and-go").

How this book is organized

The text is divided into four major sections. The first section is an overview of the mechanics of hold'em and the types of games you will encounter. The second section is the real meat of the book, describing how to play before the flop, on the flop, and after the flop. The third section covers poker and computers, including poker software, playing poker online, and no-limit sit-and-go tournaments. The fourth section contains miscellaneous topics, including a bibliography of our favorite poker books and a glossary.

We encourage you to read the book from cover to cover at least once, and then to review it (particularly the second section) regularly. You will find that the first few times you play hold'em, most of the advice in the book will flee the moment you sit down at the poker table. And conversely, the first couple of times you read the book, little of it will make sense. But as you go back and forth between the book and the table, each will become more understandable.

Vocabulary

Poker, like most pursuits, has its own vocabulary. We make an effort to introduce terms to you before using them, but if you come across something you don't understand, look it up in the glossary at the back of the book (page 257).

One final caveat

Playing poker well, like playing the resophonic guitar, writing an evocative paragraph, or successfully teaching nine-year-old boys, demands study and practice. If these activities could be done by following a simple formula, many people would do them. However, if you spoke to Jerry Douglas, Sharyn Mc-

Crumb,[5] or Robert McEwan,[6] they would tell you that they practiced incessantly to master their craft. You might be surprised to learn that the best poker players have probably "practiced" more hours than any of the distinguished people mentioned above.

We have literally worn the bindings off our best poker books reading and rereading them. We have also invested thousands of hours in playing poker. We hope you will do the same on your journey toward poker excellence.

Acknowledgments

While only my name appears as the author, this book could not have been written without the assistance and ideas of Roy Hashimoto. Among other things, he was the first person I've heard formalize the concepts of "implicit collusion" and the "dominated hand" — both incredibly powerful ideas in low-limit poker games. I believe that Roy has extraordinary insight into poker theory; despite pleading from both myself and the publisher, he chose not to have his name appear as a co-author of this book. My frequent use of the editorial "we" is intended to convey Roy's participation in this project.

My experience with low-limit hold'em has been largely gathered at San Francisco Bay area cardrooms, and I am indebted to all the players there, good and bad, who make around-the-clock poker a reality in my town. It's worth noting here that California cardrooms have been smoke-free for over six years and the dire predictions of their demise have not come true. Other states, take heed.

In previous editions of this book, I mentioned the Internet forums where I learned some of my early poker lessons and met many future poker buddies and true friends. Sadly, many of the poker forums seem to have fallen victim to the same "signal to

---

[5]I have lost not an iota of esteem for the people who were listed here in the first two editions. It was simply time to honor some other heroes of mine. If you don't recognize their names, please Google them. You will be glad you did.

[6]Robert McEwan was my fourth grade teacher at the Landon School in Bethesda, Maryland during 1966-1967. He instilled in me a love for the written and spoken word. He read Homer's *Odyssey* to his classes and had us transfixed. He, and any teacher who lights a fire in his or her students, is my hero.

noise ratio" problem that plagues all electronic meeting places. The good news is that the lessons I learned there and the friends that I met have stayed with me, and I am deeply grateful for both.

Chuck Weinstock of ConJelCo unhesitatingly said "Yes" when I suggested a book, even though I'd never before written one — I am grateful for that vote of confidence.

Over the years, I have met some wonderful people through poker, and am proud to call many of them friends. If I start trying to list them all, this chapter will run far too long, and I'll be sure to leave an important name out. These people know who they are and know how much they mean to me personally.

Barry Tanenbaum has been making a comfortable retirement income beating the $30-$60 hold'em games in Las Vegas. He is a highly respected columnist for Card Player magazine, and has an almost full-time poker coaching schedule. He agreed to review the text for the third edition, and corrected some suboptimal thinking on my part. I am indebted to Barry for his technical assistance on this edition, and even more so for his years of friendship to me.

I have to say something about my coworkers at PokerStars.com. They have been wonderful to me and given me a great introduction to poker as a business rather than a pastime. Again, there are too many names to list individually, but I am inexcusably fortunate to work with all of them.

For the third edition, my publisher, Chuck Weinstock, suggested that it was time to let an editor review the text. Somehow he found a true angel of the blue pencil, Sarah Jennings. Sarah can spot a misplaced comma at a hundred meters, and yet happily permitted me flights of grammatical whimsy when it helped the end result. This edition is better edited and better organized than either of the prior two, thanks to her work. Of course, if some error slipped past her, the blame sits squarely on me, not her.

I have benefited immeasurably from the great poker writers — you can, too (see page 253 for a complete list of valuable references). Read the books that I recommend, then play some, thinking about what you learned. Then reread the books.

My first poker lessons (as well as those in craps, roulette, and blackjack) came from my father, who, to the best of my knowledge, has never played any of those games for money. He believed them to be a good way to teach me about numbers, counting, and percentages. My mother, perhaps to counteract this education, gave me an object lesson in gambling while on a camping trip when I was five. Standing in a Nevada laundromat, she showed me a nickel (which I knew to be exchangeable for a candy bar) and dropped it into a slot machine, explaining that I would get no value for the nickel. Of course, the slot machine spewed forth a couple of dollars' worth of nickels. To both of them, I am grateful for gambling lessons, and much more that I can never repay.

Finally, and most importantly, I come to my extraordinary family: Lisa, David, and John Haupert. Lisa and I were married seven years ago, and she brought to the marriage David (now 22) and John (now 18). I was privileged to adopt David at the beginning of last year, and I adopted John just a couple of months before we went to press. Traveling, scuba diving, playing music, and just sharing time together with all of them is my greatest joy in life.

Disclaimer

I strongly believe that the information in this book is correct. However, neither I nor any other poker writer can guarantee results at the tables. You, your opponents, and your cards are responsible for that.

Another disclaimer

At this writing (autumn of 2004), I am the poker room manager for PokerStars.com — a leading provider of online poker. It is my full-time job, and my primary source of income. Obviously, I believe that PokerStars is the best site on the Internet, and I'm extremely proud of my association with them. But this is the first time that I'm working on this book as a poker industry insider, and you, the reader, should be aware of that.

LHJ
April 2005

Conventions Used in this Book

Throughout this book, we use the following notation to describe various hold'em hands — both general classes and specific:

Rank The rank of a card is represented as a single number or upper case letter: A, 2, 3, 4, 5, 6, 7, 8, 9, T, J, Q, K.

Suit The suits are represented with their symbols: ♣, ♦, ♥, ♠

Starting Cards Two card hold'em starting hands are shown as two character pairs. Since the specific suit doesn't matter, we show whether the two cards are suited or not with a lower case 's' or 'o' ("offsuit"). For example, "T8o" is ten-eight offsuit; "J9s" is jack-nine of the same suit. A card whose rank is unimportant is shown as an 'X'. For instance, AXs is an ace and any other card of the same suit.

Specific Hands Specific hands where suit is important are shown as hyphen-separated pairs. For example, "K♠-9♦" is the king of spades and nine of diamonds; "T♥-T♣" is the ten of hearts and the ten of clubs.

Ranges Sometimes we will specify a range of hands that you can play before the flop. For instance, we might use the range "KJs-T8s" when talking about hands with a single gap between the rank of the cards. This example would refer to the hands KJs, QTs, J9s, and T8s.

14

Section I

Hold'em: The Game

Hold'em Fundamentals

Hold'em (or more properly, "Texas Hold'em") is a deceptively simple poker game because only two of the cards you play are exclusively yours. The rest are shared with the other players.

Play of the hand

Each player is dealt two cards face down. These two cards are the only ones that are exclusively his.[1] There is a round of betting. Then the dealer burns a card (discards it face down onto the table) and deals three cards face up in the center of the table. These three cards are called the "flop" — they are community cards that are shared by all players. There is a second round of betting. The dealer burns another card and turns a fourth community card face up. This card is called the "turn." There is a third round of betting. The dealer then burns another card and deals the fifth and final community card face up. This card is called the "river." There is a fourth and final round of betting.

If more than one player is left in the hand after the final round of betting, there is a showdown. Each player makes the best five card poker hand he can using his two hidden cards and the five "board" cards (the flop plus the turn and river). He may use two, one, or zero of his hidden cards to make his hand. If he uses neither of his two cards, he chooses to "play the board," and the best he can do is tie all other remaining players.

---

[1] Throughout this book, we use male pronouns and possessives. This is not an attempt to slight female dealers, players, or readers. The material in this text is difficult enough without confusing the sentence structure.

Betting formats

There are two common betting formats in limit hold'em:

"Structured" games have a fixed amount that a player may bet or raise on each betting round. Typically, this is the same amount on the first two betting rounds, and then twice that amount on the last two rounds. For instance, a $3-$6 game would have $3 bets and raises before and after the flop, then $6 bets and raises after the turn and river cards. We use this $3-$6 game as an example throughout the book.

"Spread-limit" games permit a player to bet any amount within a certain range on each betting round. For instance, a common spread-limit format is $2-$6, wherein a player may bet or raise as little as $2 or as much as $6 on each betting round. However, a raise must be at least as large as any previous bet or raise in that round. Therefore, if somebody bets $5, any subsequent raise on that betting round must be at least $5. Another common spread-limit format increases the range on later betting rounds. For instance, a $4-$4-$8-$8 game has bets and raises between $1 and $4 on the first two rounds. On the last two betting rounds, players may bet or raise anything from $1 to $8.[2]

Public cardrooms and casinos

In public cardrooms and casinos, hold'em is played with 9 to 11 players. A house dealer sits in the center of one side of a long table. His job is to deal the cards, determine the winner(s) of the hand, collect the house rake or time charge, and run the game. He is *not* a player in the game.

A "dealer button" is placed in front of one player. It is a white acrylic disk labeled "DEALER." The person with the button is the nominal dealer. The cards are dealt starting one to his left, and he acts last on all betting rounds except the first. This player is often referred to as "the button."

---

[2]Spread-limit hold'em is all but gone. You may find it dealt as a very small beginner's game in some casinos, but don't go looking for it. It does not, to my knowledge, exist online at this writing.

Hold'em games rarely have an ante paid by each player. Nevertheless, in any poker game there must be some seed money in the pot. Therefore, the first player to the left of the button puts in a forced bet called a "blind." More specifically, his blind is called the "small blind" and is a fraction of a full bet (typically $1 or $2 in a $3-$6 game). The player to *his* left puts in another forced bet called the "big blind" — a full $3 bet in our example. Spread-limit games often have just a single blind, one position to the left of the button.

Because the first two players have already acted (by putting in blind bets), the player one to the left of the big blind is the first with any choices on the pre-flop betting round. He may fold, call the $3 bet, or raise the bet $3 (now forcing other players to call $6 if they wish to continue). Each player in turn has this choice with one exception: there is a maximum of three or four raises per betting round.[3] Thus, after the maximum number of raises, a player may only call or fold.

The blind bets put in by the first two players are "live blinds." When the action gets back around to them, they have the same choices as the other players except they already have a full or partial bet in the pot. For instance, when the betting gets to the small blind, if there has been no raise and he has posted a $1 blind, he needs to add only $2 to complete his bet. However, he may fold, or raise by putting in $5. The big blind already has a full bet in the pot, and if there has been no raise, he can call without putting more money in, or raise the bet $3 to a total of $6.

On each round of betting after the flop, the player to the left of the button acts first and may either check (choose not to bet) or bet. In the $3-$6 game, he is restricted to betting $3. In a spread-limit game, he may bet any amount in the valid range. The betting round proceeds from there.

When the fourth round of betting is completed (after the river card), the dealer determines the winner of the pot and pushes him

---

[3]There is often an exception to the raise limit rule: if only two players are in the pot, they may raise each other until one of them is out of chips.

the chips. If two or more players have equivalent hands (suits do not matter), the dealer splits the chips equally among them. Then he moves the button one position clockwise, shuffles the deck, and deals the next hand.

Time collection and rake

The cardroom has to make money somehow; the two common ways are taking "time" payments and "raking" the pot.

If the house takes "time" payments, it either collects a fixed amount (generally $5-6) from each player every half hour, or requires the player on the button to put up a fixed amount ($3 is common). Either way, the money is removed from the table and dropped down a collection slot by the dealer.

In cardrooms where the pot is raked, the dealer removes a specified amount of money from each pot. A common rake in low-limit games is 10% of the pot, with a maximum of $3 or $4.

In online games, the pot is always raked rather than having a time payment taken.[4]

---

[4]See the chapter "Rakes and Tokes" beginning on page 233 for more information on rakes.

Reading the Board

As a hold'em player, you must be able to read the community cards (the "board") and recognize how your hand compares with other possible hands; in particular, the *best* possible hand (known as the "nuts"). For example, if the board is

the nuts is an ace-high spade flush. If you have A♠-7♠ in your hand, you know that you have the best possible hand and will win the pot. Now the only interesting question is how to get lots of your opponents' money *into* the pot. If you have Q♠-T♠, you have the second best possible hand. Your hand is still very good, but anybody with the A♠ and another spade beats you.

If the board has a pair on it, then a full house or four-of-a-kind ("quads") is possible. For a board of

the absolute nuts is four kings. However, if you have K9 in your hand, the worst that you can do is to split the pot with one other player who has exactly the same hand. You've eliminated the possibility of four kings because you have one, and your kings full of nines is the biggest full house possible.

You need to study many hold'em boards until you can spot the nuts (and the next couple of best hands) almost immediately.

Playing Considerations
Before the Flop

This chapter is not going to be easy.

There, you're warned. This is the first chapter in which we actually talk about *how* to play low-limit hold'em. You will have to read, study, and reread this chapter and many others in the book to get full value from them. It will be difficult, but it will be rewarding.

Your decision to call, raise, or fold before the flop must be based on several factors. Among the most important are:

- Your cards.
- Your position.
- Your relative position.
- How much money you must invest initially.
- The number of players in the hand.
- How your opponents play.

If you ignore *any* of these factors when making your first playing decision, you are not likely to be a winning hold'em player.

Your cards

Starting hands (the two cards that are unique to your hand) in hold'em fall into some natural categories. You will learn that hands in different categories do well in different situations, so you need to understand and remember these categories.

Pocket Pairs: two cards that are a pair, for example, "pocket 9's." Since the difference in value between pocket aces and pocket deuces is so huge, we will separate the pocket pairs into three sub-categories: aces down through jacks are "big" pairs, tens through sevens are "medium," and sixes through twos are "little" pocket pairs. These subcategories are, of course, somewhat arbitrary, but this is a reasonable division.

Big Cards: two "big" cards, ace through jack. A♣-Q♦ and K♥-J♦ are examples of *offsuit* big cards. A♥-K♥ and K♠-Q♠ are examples of *suited* big cards.

Connectors: two cards one apart in rank. They have the ability to make straights and, if suited, flushes and straight flushes. Examples are T♦-9♦ and 6♣-5♠. Note that QJs has the distinction of being both "Big Cards" and a "Suited Connector." We sometimes include in this group the lesser quality hands with gaps between the ranks. For instance, 9♠-7♠ is a suited "one-gap." T♣-7♣ is a suited "two-gap."

Suited Aces and Kings: fairly self-explanatory. Examples are A♠-8♠, K♥-9♥. Of course, a suited ace is much stronger than a suited king because if you make a flush with it, you have the nut flush, whereas the king high flush can be beaten by the ace high flush. Having an ace high flush is *much* better than having a king high flush. Having a king high flush is only a *little* better than having a queen high flush.

Believe it or not, even if you chose to play only hands that are in these categories, you would be playing too many hands. Some of them are not strong enough to play in certain positions and some of them (32s comes to mind) are generally not strong enough to play *anywhere*. However, many of your opponents will play every hand that fits into the above categories, and a lot more as well.

Your position

Your position is simply where you are in relation to the button. Being on the button is the best position because you will act last in all but the first betting round. Being one to the left of the button is then the worst position.

Position is perhaps the most undervalued[1] component of good hold'em play. It's easy to see that bigger cards are better, suited is better than non-suited, and if there is raising going on, you need a stronger hand to play. However, many (if not most) low-limit hold'em players make their playing decisions without considering their position. *If you play without careful attention to your position, your bankroll will suffer.*

By acting after other players, you know what they will do (check, bet, etc.) before they know what you will do on a given betting round; this gives you an advantage. For instance, suppose you have a very strong hand. If your opponent acts before you and bets, then you raise. If he checks, you bet. Regardless of his action, you get the maximum amount of money in the pot. On the other hand, if you're first to act, then you must decide between betting immediately, hoping he will call, or trying to check-raise. If you check with the intent of raising and he checks too, you have lost the bet you would have made had you bet and he called.

Here's another example of the importance of position. Suppose you have 55 as your starting hand. If you are the first to act before the flop, you shouldn't call. We will cover this in detail shortly, but you need a lot of opponents to play small pairs. Suppose you call with your 55 in early position. If the next player to your left raises and scares out the other players, you now wish you hadn't called the original bet. However, suppose you are on the button. If somebody raises early and limits the pot to two players, you fold, knowing you're doing the right thing. But if six players call in front of you, you can call with your fives. Simply being closer to the button means you have more information about how many opponents you will have, enabling you to play this hand.

There is one aspect of position that is perhaps not as important in low-limit hold'em as it is in the higher limits. In tough

---

[1]That is, position is very undervalued by the average recreational player. Strong hold'em players base their game heavily on position, almost as much as on the cards they play.

hold'em games, when the flop doesn't hit[2] anybody, the player last to act can often bet and win the pot immediately. Because of the number of "calling stations" that are often in a lower limit game, it's unlikely you'll be able to do that. However, good position is still vitally important, and you must consider it at all times.

For the purposes of this text, we will consider a nine-player table. We'll declare the first three positions to the left of the big blind "early position," the next two "middle position," and the last two (including the button) "late position."[3] Of course, you'll need to adjust this for the exact number of players at your table. When doing so, tend to err on the side of caution; if you can't decide if it's early or middle position, call it "early." Also, since the blinds have to act first on all rounds after the flop, you should consider those early position for post-flop purposes.

Your relative position

There is another aspect of position to consider — let's call it "relative position." It is where you sit in relation to specific other players at the table. Obviously, your position with respect to the button will change as it moves around the table. Your relative position to another player will be less volatile. For instance, if you sit immediately on a player's left, then you'll act after him on every hand with the exception of ones on which he has the button. If you sit directly opposite him at the table, you will act before and after him equally often.

If there is a player who is very aggressive and raises a lot, you'd like to be to his left. That way, you'll see those raises coming before you act and can drop your marginal hands. If you sit to his right, too often you call one bet only to have him raise behind you and now you wish you'd saved the first bet.

---

[2]The flop is said to "hit" you if it contains cards you can use. If you have A♠-K♠ and the flop comes A♦-7♣-4♥, it has hit you. If it comes Q♠-J♠-10♦, it has clobbered you over the head. If it comes 8♥-7♥-6♥, it has missed you completely.

[3]For a ten-handed game, add one seat to "middle" position. So you'd have three early position seats, three middle, and two late.

If, however, that player almost always bets and raises (let's say 90-95% of the time), then you want to have him on *your* left. Because he'll be initiating action so frequently by betting or raising, you'll effectively act last after he has started the action. For instance, this gives you the opportunity to check-raise the entire table when you make a strong hand. Remember, for this to be correct, that particular opponent must be almost guaranteed to bet or raise when given the chance. Otherwise, keep him to your right.

In general, you'd like to have loose-passive players to your left.[4] They behave predictably so you're more willing to have them act after you. You will have an easier time predicting what they'll do, and will make the right play more often.

You may even want to move into an empty seat that gives you better position with respect to certain players.[5]

Note: positional concepts are not easy but they are important. After you've read the entire book, come back and read this section again — it will make more sense.

How much money you must invest initially

The obvious reason a player raises is that he has a strong hand. If you are playing in a pot that has been raised one or more times, there is a much better chance that you are up against strong hands, and are more likely to make a second best hand. You need a stronger hand to play in a raised pot.

Also, lots of raising before the flop reduces your implied odds. That's money not currently in the pot that you plan to win if you make your desired hand. As an example, consider playing a small pair (such as pocket fours) before the flop. You call with the pair, hoping to flop a set.[6] If you don't flop a set, you will fold. You would like to pay one bet rather than four to see the flop

---

[4]See the chapter "Player Stereotypes" beginning on page 222 for more information about loose-passive players.

[5]Mason Malmuth's book *Gambling Theory and Other Topics* contains an excellent discussion of where you want to sit in relation to various kinds of players.

with this hand. The amount of money you'll win after the flop (assuming you make your set) will be about the same regardless of the amount you invested pre-flop. Thus, if you must call lots of raises pre-flop, you are paying a higher percentage of your anticipated earnings before you've made your hand.

You must consider the possibility of a raise *behind* you when deciding what to play. This is one of the reasons that position is so vitally important. When you decide to play a hand before the flop, you *know* only what has happened in front of you. You have to suspect/guess what is going to happen behind you and play accordingly. Obviously, if you have reason to believe that there will be one or more raises behind you, you need a stronger hand to play.

The number of players in the hand

Again, this is a widely ignored factor, which you are *not* going to ignore.

Certain kinds of hands do well against a small number of opponents. These are hands that can win a pot with little or no help from the board — big pocket pairs and big cards. With a pair of pocket kings, you can often win a pot, betting all the way, without improving that pair. However, as the number of players in the hand goes up, you run a much larger chance of having a little two pair or freak straight beat you. The same holds true for AK, but you probably need to get an ace or king on the flop.

Conversely, some hands are "drawing" hands and need significant help from the board. However, if that help comes, they can turn into very big hands that you are happy to play against a lot of players. For instance, A♦-7♦ is not a very good hand on its own. Even if an ace flops, you could be in big trouble because of your low kicker. However, if you make a diamond flush, it's the nuts if there isn't a pair on the board,[7] and you're delighted to have lots of company in the hand with you. Since these drawing

---

[6]A "set" is a pair in your hand and a third card of that rank on the board. It is still three of a kind, but this is more desirable than three of a kind where two of your rank are on the board.

hands need help that comes somewhat rarely (for instance, with a suited ace you will only flop two more of your suit about 11% of the time), you need lots of players in the hand to provide the pot odds to call.

Thus, in general you'd like to play your big cards and high pairs against a small number of players and your smaller pairs and suited cards against many opponents.

I want to say something about the monster pairs (AA-QQ) here. Some players believe that the reason you raise with these hands is to get other people out of the pot. In fact, with aces, you'd love to have everybody at the table in for the maximum number of bets. Of course, as the number of players in the pot increases, your chance of winning the pot goes down. But that is more than overcome by the larger pot size — your *expected value* increases.

How your opponents play

You have to know something about how your opponents play to play your cards optimally. For instance, suppose there is a player on your immediate right, and he hasn't played a hand in 20 minutes. He's currently under the gun (first to act before the flop) and he raises. You have KQo — what do you do? You fold. Suppose, however, that the player on your right has raised the last eight straight hands. He raises for the ninth straight time (again, under the gun) and you have the same KQo. What do you do? You might well re-raise here (if you thought that would limit the field). Concepts such as this are crucial if you want to succeed at poker.

Playing behind a raiser

You'll see that I recommend playing very tightly behind a raiser, even one who raises too much. Many players who would be winning players are losers because they call too many raises cold.

---

[7]For the nit-picking reader, it is true that the ace high flush can be beaten on an unpaired board if somebody makes a straight flush. One takes one's chances.

So, the mantra for what to do when it's raised in front of you: "I'm looking for a reason to get out of this hand."

When it's raised after you call or raise

Sometimes you'll call and then somebody will raise behind you. Or you'll raise and somebody will re-raise. Quite often when this happens (particularly when you've called), your thought will be, "Oh bother — now I wish I hadn't called in the first place," because you really didn't want to pay two bets to see the flop with that particular hand. This may well be true, but at that point, it's *rarely* correct for you to fold. You are now getting much better pot odds on that second bet than you were on the first, and even though you would have folded for two bets cold in the first place, you must now pay the second bet "on the installment plan."

The exception to this rule is if it is raised twice or more after you've invested a single bet, or you fear that that is about to happen. In that case, you need to review the situation (your cards, the pot odds, your position, etc.) more carefully. It may be best to abandon that single bet and avoid further trouble.

Last action

This is another crucially important concept, not only pre-flop, but on every betting round. If your calling a bet will end the betting round, you can play much more liberally than you can otherwise. This is simply because you don't have to fear raises behind you. For instance, you have 7♣–5♣ on the big blind. The first person in raises, and gets three callers. It's fine for you to call there because you "close the betting."[8] But if the action went call, call, raise, call, and now it's your turn, you should fold. The first two callers will *almost* always just call the second bet, but when one of them decides to re-raise, you're paying too much for your hand pre-flop. And if the original raiser makes it four bets, you have a miserable situation.

---

[8]To the best of my knowledge, Mike Caro publicly coined this term.

When you're thinking about calling (on *any* betting round) with a marginal hand, be much more willing to do so if you have last action.

Starting hand requirements

My starting hand requirements have changed with each new edition of the book as I've learned more about the game. By and large, they've gotten tighter. But it's important to understand that this set of starting hand requirements is just a beginning. Honestly, I don't believe it matters much whether you follow this set of starting hands, Sklansky and Malmuth, Krieger, or any other intelligent poker writer. The areas in which the various thinking writers disagree probably account for a tiny fraction of your results, either way.[9] For instance, I don't think it will affect your long-term results a great deal if you do or don't play QTs for a single bet in middle position. Of course, in the short term, you might flop a costly second-best hand with it, or turn a monster-crushing straight flush, but over the course of your poker career, I doubt you'd be able to tell financially whether you played it three from the big blind or not. On the other hand, if you choose to play J6o there, or don't routinely get a lot of money in the pot with KK in that position, your results will suffer dramatically.

Also, game conditions can dramatically affect what you should play where. If a good hold'em player is asked, "Can you play AJo in early position?" the answer will be, "It depends." On how well his opponents play, how tight they are, what the current texture of the game is, his table image, and so on.

So, treat all of the starting hand information as guidelines and not gospel. If in doubt, fold — another hand will be along shortly, and you may well be avoiding an expensive mistake.

---

[9]There is a principle in poker that I call the 'Angelo Axiom,' named for poker pro and writer Tommy Angelo. It states that the longer a point of poker strategy is argued, the less it really matters what the player does in that situation. I believe that the Angelo Axiom is tremendously accurate.

Be extra conservative if you're a novice

When you're new to any sport or activity, you start out slowly and become more adventurous as you gain experience and knowledge. Hold'em is no different. When you're first learning the game, avoid the lower end of any of the hand rankings. For instance, you'll see that I say you can play J9s and 76s in late position if enough players are in. If you're new at this, don't bother. You can make plenty of money *not* playing them, and they may cost you money when you're still in the beginning stages of your career. In fact, you can be an extremely successful hold'em player *never* playing those hands.

Summary

We've discussed the important factors you must consider when you decide whether to get involved in a pot. In the next four chapters, we'll cover what you can play pre-flop and how to play it. As you read those chapters, refer back to this one to see how the decisions are based on the above considerations.

Odds, Pot Odds, and Implied Odds

To play poker well, you must understand the terms *odds*, *pot odds*, and *implied odds*. Let's be sure that you grasp each term thoroughly before we go on.

Probability and odds

"Probability" is the likelihood of an event happening. It is a number between zero and one, and is often expressed as a percentage. For instance, a .70 probability of rain today is the same as a 70% chance of rain.

"Odds" are another way of expressing probability and are more applicable to games of chance such as poker. Odds are shown as a pair of numbers separated by a colon; the pair represents a ratio between the probability of an event happening and its not happening. Being somewhat whimsical, we could say (from our example above) that rain is a 7:3 "favorite" today. That is, the odds of rain are 7 to 3 in its favor; for every seven times it rains on a day like today, there will be three dry days. The opposite of favorite is "underdog" (or "dog" for short). If you say, "That team is a 5:2 underdog," you mean that for every two times they win in this situation, they will lose five.

What do odds mean to betting? Let's consider the weather forecast above. You and a friend decide to bet on whether it will rain. Given that you know rain is a 7:3 favorite, what is a "fair" bet? If you choose to bet on rain, and your friend bets on no rain, you should put up $7 for each $3 he wagers. Over 10 days, it will probably rain seven times. You will collect $3 from your friend on each rainy day for a total of $21. On the remaining three days, it will not rain. Your friend will collect $7 from you on each dry day for a total of $21. Thus, on any given day, one of you will pay the other, but in the *long run*, you will both expect to break even. Now, suppose you can find somebody willing to put up $4 for each $7 you bet, but you know that rain is indeed a 7:3 favorite. You still lose $21 on the three dry days, but you collect $4 each of the seven rainy days for a total of $28. In 10 average days, you make a $7 profit! This book will teach you to find and exploit opportunities where you have a similar edge over your opponents.

Let's look at a hold'em example. Suppose you have flopped a heart flush draw. That is, you have two hearts in your hand, and two more come on the flop. What are the odds of making your flush on the next card (the turn)? There are a total of 13 hearts in the deck; you have seen four of them, leaving nine more. You have seen a total of five cards (your two plus three in the flop). That leaves 47 unseen cards, of which nine are the hearts you want to see. There are 38 cards that do not make your flush and nine that do; the odds are 38:9 "against." You are a 38:9 (slightly worse than 4:1) underdog to make your flush on the turn.

Pot odds

Pot odds are the odds being offered to you by the pot compared to the amount of money you must invest in it. For instance, suppose after the river card is turned up, there is $30 in the pot. Your opponent bets $6. The pot now has $36 in it, and you have to call $6 to see his hand. You are getting *pot odds* of 6:1. You will also hear the expression "the pot is *laying* you 6:1." Now your choice is (relatively) easy: if you are no worse than a 6:1 underdog to win the pot, you call the $6; otherwise you fold.

Pot odds also apply to draws. Suppose you have a draw that is a 3:1 underdog to be made. For you to call a bet, there should be at least three times as much money in the pot as the amount you must call. Of course, that includes any bets that precede your call. For instance, if the pot contains $15 and your opponent bets $6, the pot now contains $21 and is laying you 3.5:1. Since you are only a 3:1 underdog, you can call.

Implied odds

Going a step beyond pot odds are "*implied odds*." More accurately, they might be called implied pot odds. When you compute pot odds, you can only consider the money that's already in the pot. The concept of implied odds lets you ask the question, "If I make the hand I'm drawing to, how much more money will I win than what's already in the pot?"

For example, suppose you have a flush draw with one card left to come. You know you are about a 4:1 underdog to make your flush. There is $16 in the pot, and your opponent bets $6. The pot (now $22) is laying you about 3.7:1, but you're a 4:1 dog to make your flush. According to strict pot odds, you can't call. However, suppose you're "sure" that your opponent will call a $6 bet on the river if you make your flush. Now you can act as if the pot contains $28 (what it currently contains plus the $6 more you will win if you make your flush). You can make the $6 call with your flush draw.

Of course, when considering pot odds or implied odds for a draw, you must be "sure" that you will win the pot if you make your draw. If you're not sure, then the pot must lay you a higher price to make your draw correct. Also, when considering implied odds, you must be just as sure that your opponent will call your bet after you have made your hand.

Your money, the pot's money

Poker players often get confused about to whom money belongs. They say, "I have a lot of money in the pot." This is a fallacious concept. Once the money is in the pot, you should no longer care whether it came from your stack or those of your opponents. The only interesting question is whether the pot is laying you the correct price for a draw or whatever.

Don't worry about how much money you have contributed to a pot during a hand when deciding if a call is correct. The pot odds (or implied odds) will answer that question and are unaffected by your past contributions to the pot.

Some odds you should know

You are a 220:1 dog to be dealt a pair of aces (or any other specific pair). You are a 16:1 dog to be dealt a pocket pair.

You are a 3.3:1 dog to be dealt two suited cards.

You are a 7.5:1 underdog to flop trips (three of a kind) if you hold a pocket pair.

If you have an ace and a king in your hand, you are a 2.1:1 underdog to flop at least one ace or king.

If you have a pair of pocket kings, it's about 4:1 in your favor against a single ace showing on the flop without a king.

If you have two suited cards, you are a 7.5:1 dog to get at least two more of your suit on the flop.

If you flop a flush draw (four to a flush), you are a 4.2:1 dog to make your flush on the turn. You're a 4.1:1 dog to make it on the river if you don't make it on the turn (you've seen one more card that's not your suit). Once you've flopped four to a flush, you're a 1.9:1 dog to make it by the river.

If you flop an open-end straight flush draw (e.g., you have T♠-9♠ and the flop comes 8♠-7♠-2♣), you are a 1.2:1 *favorite* to make a straight or better by the river.

An open-end straight draw is about a 4.9:1 dog on *either* the turn or the river. If you flop an open end straight draw, you are a 2.2:1 underdog to make it by the river. With a gutshot (inside) straight draw, you are an 11:1 dog to make your straight on the next card.

Computing odds

Computing your odds of making a draw on the next card is fairly straightforward. You simply compare the number of cards that don't make your draw to the number that do. Those are your odds. For instance, suppose you have J♥-9♥ and the flop comes

T♦-5♠-Q♣. Any eight or king will give you a straight;[1] you have eight outs.[2] What are the odds of making your straight on the next card? Of 47 unseen cards, eight make your straight, 39 do not. Thus you are a 39:8 (almost 5:1) underdog to make the straight on the turn.

---

[1]It's worth noting that the straight you make with the king is not the nuts. At that point, AJ is the nuts.

[2]An "out" is a card that will make your hand, and presumably win the pot for you. This term, and many others, are defined in the glossary.

The Typical Low-Limit Hold'em Game

When you sit down in a low-limit hold'em game, you are likely to find a broad range of poker experience and knowledge. Some players will be retirees who use the game as their social club and book fifty hours or more there each week. Others will have a discreet crib sheet in front of them showing the ranking of poker hands. Most of your opponents will lie somewhere in between — they'll be working folks who come down to the club for relaxation and a good poker game.

Of course, when you play on the Internet, it's essentially impossible to know exactly who your opponents are.[1] But you can be sure that you're encountering an astonishing array of people from all walks of life and from all over the world. That, in itself, makes hold'em on the Internet a fascinating experience.

Low-limit games are often only half-jokingly called "no fold'em hold'em." You will often see seven or eight people at a nine-person table call to see the flop. Furthermore, many players will stay around after the flop with very weak or almost hopeless draws. In some cases, they *know* that they're taking the worst of the odds, but they get a special charge from catching those miracle cards and beating very strong hands.

---

[1]Needless to say, the player "SexySusie" with the image of an attractive blonde may well be a Pittsburgh iron worker named Roscoe.

Unlike in higher limit games, you are not likely to encounter any professional players in your low-limit hold'em game; your opponents will be playing for entertainment. The most obvious result of this is that people want to play more hands.

The two most common kinds of games are "loose-passive" and "loose-aggressive."[2] In the former, many players pay to see the flop, but there is not much raising. In the latter scenario, there are many players for each flop, but many pots have three or four bets put in before the flop — everybody is "gambling." Note that the common thread between these two types of low-limit games is many players in each pot; this is unusual in higher limit games.

Sometimes the nature of the game will change, and it will get much tighter. When somebody raises before the flop, he may win the pot right there. A significant percentage of hands do not go past the flop. This is most common in short-handed games (ones with fewer than the regular number of players).

Low-limit versus micro-limit

The advent of online poker has made it possible for people to play hold'em for stakes that couldn't possibly be profitable for a public cardroom to spread. These games, when they first appeared, were dubbed "micro-limits" because they were lower than anything that had ever been available in public poker. Players on the Internet play $.05-$.10 (and occasionally smaller) hold'em games using the same software as is used for the $30-60 games on the site. While a $3-6 hold'em game is definitely "low-limit," a bad night in such a game can cost you perhaps $240 — definitely a sum most people would notice. But an equivalent loss (in "bet" units) for a $.05-.10 player would be $4.00, much less than the cost of a movie. Given that, the players in micro-limit games tend to be even less concerned about their calling and raising standards.

While this book will teach you to beat both the micro-limit and the traditional low-limit games, realize that they will play very

---

[2]See the chapter "Player Stereotypes" beginning on page 222 for more information about these terms.

differently. You will almost always have more people seeing the flop, and more pre-flop raises in the micro-limit games. When the money at risk amounts to only what you could find in your sofa cushions, don't expect your raises to carry much weight and don't expect others' raises to carry much information.

Expect to see all but one or two players seeing every flop,[3] and showdowns at the river routinely involving 4-5 people. Whenever we talk about "lots of people" being in the pot, the micro-limit games are likely to be the perfect example of that.

---

[3]Note that at online sites such as PokerStars.com, it's easy to see, for each game, what percentage of players are seeing the flop.

Quiz on
Preliminary Chapters

Congratulations! You've made it through the first section. To help cement the important points in your mind, please take this quiz, and *write down the answers*. Then check your answers against the answers on page 42. If you get any answers wrong, go back and re-read the text until you understand the answer to each question.

1. Should you read this book if you've never played poker?

2. What level of games do we define as "low-limit"?

3. How many cards in a hold'em hand are uniquely yours?

4. How many betting rounds are there in a hold'em hand, and when do they take place?

5. How many cards does the "flop" contain?

6. How many cards do you use from your unique cards to make your best five card poker hand?

7. Under the conventions of this book, what hold'em hands do the following represent?
    a) 88
    b) QJo
    c) T9s
    d) AXo

e) J♠-T♣

f) K♦-4♦

g) AQs-J9s

8. What is the best possible hand (the "nuts") given these boards? What is the second best possible hand?

a) A♦-K♥-6♠-4♠-T♣

b) 7♥-4♠-3♦-9♥-J♠

c) A♣-5♠-T♥-2♣-9♠

d) 3♣-J♣-Q♥-6♣-3♦

e) 6♦-9♦-9♥-K♠-5♦

f) T♣-5♥-J♦-Q♠-K♣

g) J♠-2♣-Q♦-4♥-7♣

h) 4♥-6♠-8♥-J♦-9♥

9. Suppose you have the hand 8♥-8♦. On the turn, the board is 6♣-8♠-7♦-9♥. What are your odds of making a full house or better on the river?

10. From the previous question, suppose just you and a single opponent are left in the pot on the turn. He bets $6, and you are persuaded that he has a straight. Of course, if you make a full house (or better), you will win the pot. How much money has to be in the pot after he bets for your call to be correct?

11. Suppose you believe that your opponent will check and call your $6 bet if you *do* make a full house. Then how much money should be in the pot for you to call, trying to make a full house or quads?

Answers to Quiz on Preliminary Chapters

1. No, you should read *Fundamentals of Poker* by Malmuth and Loomis, or *Poker for Dummies* by Harroch and Krieger first.

2. $1-$2 up through $5-$10 or $6-$12. Spread-limit games from $1-$3 up to $2-$10.

3. Two.

4. Four. Pre-flop, after the flop, after the turn, after the river.

5. Three.

6. Two, one, or zero. If you use zero, the best you can do is split the pot with all players remaining in the hand.

7. a) A pair of 8's.

    b) A queen and a jack of different suits (offsuit).

    c) A ten and a nine of the same suit (suited).

    d) An ace and any other card of a different suit.

    e) The jack of spades and the ten of clubs.

    f) The king of diamonds and the four of diamonds.

    g) The range of suited one-gap hands including ace-queen suited, king-jack suited, queen-ten suited, and jack-nine suited.

8. a) QJ for the ace high straight; next best is three aces.

b) T8 for the jack high straight; next best is 56 for the seven high straight.

c) 34 for the five high straight; next best is three aces.

d) Four threes; next best is queens full of threes.

e) 8♦-7♦ for the nine high straight flush; next best is four nines.

f) Any ace for the ace high straight; next best is any nine for the king high straight.

g) Three queens; next best is three jacks. Note: three queens is the lowest possible hand that can be the nuts when all five board cards are dealt.

h) A♥ and any other heart for the ace high heart flush; next best is K♥ and another heart for the king high flush.

9.   To improve to a full house or better, you need the board to pair. There are three each of sixes, sevens, and nines, plus the last eight in the deck. That makes a total of ten "outs" that give you a full house or better. Since you've seen six cards (two in your hand, four on the board), there are 46 unseen cards, ten of them good for you. Thus your odds of improving (making a full house or quads) on the river are 36:10 (3.6:1) against.

10. You are about a 3.6:1 underdog when your opponent bets $6. Thus for you to call the $6 bet, the pot must contain 3.6 x $6 (about $22) when you call. If the pot (including his last bet) is at least $22, you can call, hoping to improve on the river. If you want to squeak out the last statistical detail, note that for your opponent to have a straight, he must have either a five or a ten. Because that five or ten must be in your opponent's hand, you can remove it from your theoretical deck of remaining cards. Now you can say that you have 10 outs from 45 (instead of 46) unseen cards, making you a 3.5:1 underdog. The pot must contain $21 for you to call.[1]

11.   If you are persuaded your opponent will call your $6 bet on the river, that is an extra $6 you plan to win should you improve. You are still a 3.5:1 dog, so you still need $21 total to justify your call. Subtracting the extra $6 you plan to win, the pot only had to contain $15 for you to call on the turn. Note: All these calculations were done assuming you would throw away your trips on the river if you didn't improve. If you were planning to call a bet if you *didn't* make your full house, then you are effectively calling $12 ($6 on the turn and $6 on the river). Now the pot has to be offering you better odds to call on the turn.

---

[1]Believe me, this is right. It's also not at all intuitive, and not the least bit necessary to worry about until you start posting on Internet poker forums.

Section II

Play of the Hand from Deal to Showdown

Playing Pre-Flop in Early Position

You must play <u>very</u> tightly before the flop
in early position.

If there is no raise in front of you

You can play any of the big pocket pairs in early position. With AA-JJ (and occasionally TT), raise — you have a very big hand. However, against eight random hands, your pocket aces will end up the best hand only about 35% of the time. Don't feel bad about that; if you got pocket aces on every hand (and your opponents forgot this after every hand), you would make a ton of money.

With TT-99, just *call*. The traditional reason for raising with these pairs is to reduce the number of opponents, particularly those holding a single ace or king. If raising is effective at thinning the field in your game, by all means do so. However, in low-limit games, you probably won't have much success getting singleton aces and kings to fold for a raise. Therefore, it makes more sense to see the flop cheaply.

In early position, you want unpaired cards to be huge. Raise with AKs, AKo, AQs, and AQo.

In the first edition, I was hesitant recommending a raise with AK (suited or not). That was a mistake. You should raise with AK both because you hope to limit the field to a few opponents, and to punish the dominated hands (e.g., AJ) that call behind you.

However, as you'll see in the chapter on playing the flop, you will normally need to improve your AK to win the pot.

There aren't many non-pairs that you should call with in early position. You can call with AJs, KQs, and KJs.[1]

A word about AJo: when you're new to the game, I encourage you to fold AJo in early position. Interestingly, raising AJo in early position is a bad idea. You might make hands worse than yours (e.g., AT, A9) fold, but you'll never make hands better than yours (AK, AQ) fold. So you're limiting the opposition to those hands better than yours. You can't raise with it, and calling with a marginal hand (which AJo is) in early position is not how you win money. Until you have the experience to know when you can sneak in with AJo, dump it. Note the significant difference between this hand and AJs or AQo.

If the game is loose and passive (generally 4-5 players seeing the flop for one bet each), you can shade these requirements down a little with your suited hands and (even more so) the pocket pairs. In fact, if you expect to have at least 5-6 opponents in the pot with you, you can call with *any* pair, even if it's going to cost multiple bets.[2] This is because your chances of flopping a set is a bit worse than one in seven. With that many opponents, you're getting the right pot odds to flop your set.

If there is a raise in front of you

The key idea here: "Look for a reason to fold." Even if the raiser is a hyper-aggressive lunatic, (1) hyper-aggressive lunatics get dealt KK on occasion, and (2) if somebody is holding KK behind you, you're going to be facing a third bet. So, play *very* tightly behind an early position raiser. Re-raise with AA-JJ, AKs, AKo. Maybe AQs and AQo. Don't even call with TT or AJs.[3]

---

[1]This is tighter than the first two editions recommended. I am now persuaded that there is no reason (particularly for novice players and particularly in early position) to get involved with hands weaker than these.

[2]This is not permission to call three bets cold with 44 in early position because you *hope* there will be enough players to justify your call.

Again, remember that you won't have to wait long for the next hand.[4] And while you're waiting for that next hand, ponder this sobering thought: it's a mistake to call an early position raise with KQo.

Be patient

Following these guidelines, you will play only about 1 in 12 hands you get in early position. If the game is loose-passive, then you will play about one in seven hands. Be patient and wait for the best cards; your early position handicap demands that you do so.

Summary — Early position

Raise: AA-JJ (sometimes TT). AKs-AJs, AKo, and AQo. Always re-raise with AA-JJ, AKs, and AQs. Re-raise with the others in this group if it will tend to limit the number of players in the pot.

Call one bet: TT-99, KQs-KJs. ATs and KQo if you're three beyond the big blind. If the game is very loose (5+ players seeing every flop), call with *any* pocket pair.

Fold: Everything else.

Remember: You must play *very* tightly before the flop in early position.

---

[3]Another change since the second edition. These hands just don't fare well against a legitimate early position raiser. If the first raiser raises too liberally, *and* a re-raise will thin the field, then do that. But don't call.

[4]On the Internet, the time until the next hand is almost trivially short. You would think that players would be willing to play tighter online because they don't have to wait as long for the next hand. The exact opposite seems to be true.

Playing Pre-Flop in Middle Position

As your position improves, you can start to play a few more hands, but you still have to be conservative in what you play.

Of course, you can play anything that was playable from early position.

Raising first-in vs. raising after callers

When you're playing in early position, you're often the first person putting money into the pot. And the hands that you're raising with are so strong that you don't mind raising when somebody is already in.

The further you are from the big blind, the more frequently you will have "limpers" (callers) in front of you. When that happens, tighten up your raising requirements. One of the reasons that you raise (with anything but AA-QQ) is that you'd like to win the blinds without a flop. Once somebody has called in front of you, the chances of doing that are almost nil. So then it's better to call (rather than raise) with the lower range of your raising hands.

Raising or folding when you're the first one in

As your position improves, you have a better chance of winning the blinds uncontested if you're the first player into the pot and raise. And when you limp as the first one in (particularly in middle or late position), you've basically stated, "Well, I have this hand that's too good to fold but not good enough to raise. So I guess I'll just call and see what happens."

Many extremely successful players have a "no open-limp" policy. That is, if they're the first one into the pot, then they either raise or fold. Not *all* good players take this approach, but it does clarify your plan for proceeding in the hand, and this is very helpful for new players.

As an example, suppose you are three in front of the button and have pocket sixes. It's folded to you. There are two calling stations behind you with their chips already in their hands to call. If you raise, do you suppose they'll fold? No — they'll simply put out twice as many chips. So you're likely to end up playing a small pair out of position against 2-3 opponents, which is a complete mess. It's much easier to fold and forget about it.

Conversely, if you think you may be able to get everybody out, or perhaps everybody except the calling station in the small blind, then raise. But calling here achieves nothing; don't do it.

This discussion provides good context for an extremely important point: what you do with a hand must be *strongly* tied to what happens in front of you. For instance, with 77, you might well decide, "If it's folded to me, I raise. If there are at least three callers, I call. Otherwise, I fold." This sort of thinking is crucial to profitable pre-flop play.

If there is no raise in front of you

Pocket pairs: If the game is loose (4-5 players seeing every flop), you can play any pair. Raise down to 88.[1] If you're one of the first few in, and you have a smaller pair, it's best to fold. If you have a reasonable chance of stealing the blinds, then raise. But often you don't have much chance to win the blinds without a flop and you're not getting the pot odds to flop a set. So fold.

Big cards: You can raise with the same hands you would have raised in early position, plus a few others — KJs, QJs, ATs, JTs, KQo, KJo, AJo, JTo. But the offsuit hands only deserve a raise if you're the first one in.

---

[1] Call, rather than raise, with 99-88 if there are callers in front of you.

Suited connectors: You'd like to play those against a large number of opponents since you probably need to make a straight or a flush to win. If there are three or four players in the pot before it gets to you, you can call with suited connectors down to 98s. You can also play QTs. Again, if there are just one or two players in the pot, you need to tighten up, playing only those suited connectors that have big card value, too. For instance, if two people have called in front of you, don't play suited connectors lower than JTs. But if four people have limped in, then calling with 98s is okay.[2]

If you're in a loose-passive game (at least 4-5 players seeing the flop, and almost always for one bet), you can call with any suited connector down to 76s and suited one-gaps to J9s.

Unsuited connectors: I am now persuaded that unsuited connectors are not as valuable as some people feel. Therefore, don't get involved with unsuited connectors unless they have big card value too.

That said, I want to make special mention of JT. Either suited or unsuited, it has some unique properties: it makes the most possible straights, all the straights it makes are the nuts, and when you make a straight with it you often get lots of action. That's because it makes straights with high cards, and beats big pairs, two pairs, and even sets. Don't call raises cold with it, but with a couple of people in, it's a good hand to play for one bet. Note: T9o is *much* weaker than JTo.

Suited aces: If you have at least three callers in front of you, you can call with AXs. Your suited ace will flop a flush draw (or flush) almost exactly as often as your pocket pair will turn into trips on the flop. You need plenty of people in the pot to make this call correct. You can play suited kings down to KTs. When playing these hands, remember that if the flop comes ace-high or king-high you have top pair, but might also have kicker problems — be careful.

---

[2] I say "okay." Which is better than "a bad idea" but not as good as "great." If you never played 98s, you could still make a lot of money playing hold'em.

If there is a raise in front of you

Just as in early position, you need to tighten up considerably. Not only do you have to put in two bets, you must also consider the possibility of a re-raise behind you. You can just go back to early position rules for hands that you can call. However, you can play any pair and big suited connectors down to JTs if four players are already in.

Re-raise with the same hands that we suggested re-raising with in early position. These are very big hands that justify putting more money in the pot on pure expected value.

If there have been two raises in front of you

If the pot has been raised twice or more before it gets to you, there are a couple of things to consider. First, there's a good chance that the betting will be capped. Second, you're up against at least one, if not two, big hands. Go back to those early position premium hands and rely on them. For example, you can quickly throw away pocket 10's.

In fact, it's a fine rule to say, "If it comes to me three bets cold, and I don't feel that I can cap the betting, then I'll just fold." Given that, re-re-raise with AA-QQ, AKs, and AKo. Otherwise get out.

Pocket jacks

This hand is so awkward that it gets its own subsection of the chapter. Pocket queens are a huge pair and should be played aggressively. Pocket tens are extremely vulnerable, and most players sense that and play accordingly. Pocket jacks are neither fish nor fowl. They're pretty to look at and almost impossible for new players to fold. And yet they can cost you a lot of money played improperly. Part of the problem is that an overcard will come on the flop about half the time, and then it's very difficult to know what to do.

If nobody has raised, you should always raise with JJ. Perhaps it will limit the field, and even if it doesn't, your hand is strong enough to justify putting in more money.

Your difficulty comes in dealing with three bets cold. When first drafting this subsection, I wrote two paragraphs telling you how to handle JJ when it's three bets to you. I'll now write it in one word:

Fold.

That may seem harsh, but for beginning players, it's almost certainly the correct play. And folding may well keep you out of expensive trouble trying to drag a monster pot with a marginal hand.

Summary — Middle position

You're the first one in

Raise:	The higher range of hands you were going to play anyway.
Fold:	Everything else — don't call.

One to three callers in front

Raise:	AA-TT, AKs-KQs, AQs-KJs, AJs, ATs, AKo. If just 1-2 callers in front: AQo.
Call:	99-88, JTs, QTs, QJs, AXs, KTs, JTo.

Four or more callers in front

Raise:	Same as above.
Call:	Above plus 77-22, T9s-76s, J9s.

A raise in front

Raise:	AA-JJ, AKs, AQs, AKo, AQo.
Call:	KQs-QJs, KJs, AJs. If 4+ players already in: any pair, ATs.

More than one raise in front

Raise:	AA-QQ, AKs, AKo.
Call:	Any pair if there are already 4+ players in.
Fold:	Everything else.

Playing Pre-Flop in
Late Position

*When you are in the last couple of positions to act, you
have an extraordinary advantage.*

This is where you can take some liberties with the hands you
play. Remember, in a typical low-limit game, by the time the action gets to you, a lot of players will already be in the pot.

Now you can play more speculative hands. Furthermore, you'll
act last (or second to last) in every succeeding betting round. You
can take some chances here, because you'll see how the betting
is going before you have to act.

If there is no raise in front of you

Pairs: Given that four or five players are in, play *any* pocket pair.
Again, raise with AA-88, otherwise call and look at the flop. If
you like the flop (nothing bigger than your pair) or love the flop
(you make a set), everybody has to act in front of you, and you'll
be holding the big hand. Realize that particularly for hands such
as 99 and 88, you may well need to flop a set to win. But you're
getting the right price and you're punishing players who have
limped in with junk.

If fewer than four players are in, still raise with AA-88, but just
dump the lower pairs (with the possible exception of 77). You're
not getting the right price to flop a set, you can't steal the blinds,
it's a mess; throw them away.

Big cards: You can play any two cards both ten or higher. However, remember that your unsuited big cards do *not* like lots of opponents. You can call with QJo after a lot of people are in the pot, but don't proceed past the flop unless you make top pair or a good draw.[1] But your position gives you license to play some borderline hands. Call and see how you like the flop.

Suited connectors: These are the kind of hands you like to play in late position. You can play suited connectors right down to 76s. Even the one-gaps down to 97s are okay. Two-gaps, don't bother except AJs and KTs.[2] Of course, you need plenty of people in the pot with you. If you have fewer than four callers in front, dump the lower end of the range. Again, stay away from unsuited connectors (except JTo, which I discussed previously).

The thing to remember is that you're going to need real help on the flop with these hands, and it's not going to come very often. Most of the time you play these hands, you'll be throwing them away on the flop. However, once in a while you will flop a big hand or draw with them.

Finally, don't forget what I wrote in the introduction to the book about playing the marginal hands I've mentioned. While some players make money with hands such as 76s, probably many more *lose* money with that hand because they take it further than it deserves after the flop (and/or they play it too liberally pre-flop). If you decided to just use the middle position criteria in playing connectors and gap hands, even in late position, you certainly wouldn't give up much profit, and might gain some.

Suited aces: If you have a few callers in front and no raises, you can play any suited ace and KTs-K9s. However, you must treat them like the suited connectors — if you're holding A7s, and flop just an ace, you will have to play it delicately. That is, you have essentially no kicker, and may need to abandon the hand if

---

[1] I'll define "good draw" in future chapters.

[2] In previous editions, I suggested playing more one-gap and two-gap hands. Barry Tanenbaum is right; these hands are just trouble, even with position.

there's much action. What you're really hoping for on the flop is a big flush draw (or pat flush).

Raising with medium-small pairs

If at least five people call in front of you, it's okay to occasionally (even "frequently") raise with medium-ish pairs. The reason, again, is that you're only slightly worse than a 7:1 underdog to flop a set. So if that many people are in the pot with you, it costs you nothing in expected value to raise. And perhaps you can get them to remember, "Hey — he raises with pocket sixes."

Now, suppose you do this, you don't flop a set, and they check to you on the flop. Don't do anything stupid; take your free card and your 4% chance of hitting a set on the turn. There's no law that says because you raised pre-flop you have to bet the flop.

There's no particular reason you can't do this with any pair, but just because it's so painful when you flop an under-set,[3] I wouldn't make this play with a pair smaller than 66 or 55.

If there is a raise in front of you

Playing from last position, you'll have a pretty good idea of the effect of the raise. If the raise happened in early position but a bunch of people have called it already, you know that the pot will lay you proper odds for your drawing hands. If the raise happens in late position after a lot of calls, you're probably still okay since very few players will call one bet and then throw their cards away for a single raise.[4]

You're going to get tired of hearing me say this, but I'll say it again: if there's a raise in front of you, look for an excuse to get rid of your cards. If you wouldn't call a raise cold with it in middle position, don't call a raise cold with it in late position. For instance, an early position player (whom you respect) raises, and gets called only by the biggest calling station at the table. There's no reason to play 77 or A6s here. You don't have the pot odds to

---

[3] You flop a set, and somebody flops a bigger set. It's very ugly.

[4] This intuitive behavior — to call a single raise after you've already committed one bet — is generally correct. At that point, the pot is laying you a very high price for a single bet (assuming you don't fear a re-raise).

treat the hands as drawing hands, and they're not strong enough to treat as made hands. So you fold.

Stealing the blinds

Just as we discussed for middle position, if you're the first person in, and you're going to play, raise. This may win the blinds for you; it may get you the button (if you don't already have it). At the very least, it will put your opponents on the defensive, and that's always desirable.

Again, do not take this as permission to open-raise with anything on the button. Throw away J6o without a second thought unless the blinds don't defend enough, in which case you should open-raise with any two cards. But that's usually not the case in low-limit games. Normally, they'll defend too much, so you should throw away your weaker hands and punish their looseness by raising with your better ones.

Also note: a hand in which a late position player open-raises and just the big blind defends is a very different beast from a typical multi-way pot. Any pair or draw is a pretty good hand, and top pair is a monster. This sort of hand-to-hand combat is not for most poker novices. It's more art than science, and until you're ready to learn that aspect of the game you might be better off folding all but your very big hands if you're the first person in on the button.

Summary — Late position

You're the first one in

Raise: Anything you were going to play anyway.

Fold: Everything else — don't call.

One to three callers in front

Raise: AA-TT, AKs-QJs, AQs-KJs, AJs, ATs, JTs, AKo. If just 1-2 callers in front: KQo, AQo, AJo, ATo.

Call: 77, JTs-98s, QTs-J9s, KTs, K9s, AXs, QJo-JTo, KJo-QTo, KTo.

Four or more callers in front

Raise:	Same as above. Plus occasionally pairs down to 55.
Call:	As above, plus *any* pair, 87s-76s, T8s-97s.

A raise in front

Raise:	AA-JJ, AKs, AQs, AKo, AQo
Call:	TT-99, KQs, KJs, AJs. If at least four players are already in: 88-77, ATs, QJs, A9s. If five or more players are already in: *any* pair.

Note: I've made every attempt to make the starting hand tables consistent. However, if you find an inconsistency, here's the rule: if you can play it in early position, then you can play it in middle or late position. If you can play it in middle position, then you can play it in late position.

Playing Pre-Flop in the Blind Positions

Being in the blind positions puts you in an awkward situation. You already have all or part of a bet in the pot, so you must pay less to enter the pot and you are being offered better pot odds to participate. However, you are in the worst position for the rest of the hand.

Big blind

This one is somewhat easier to consider because you already have a full bet in the pot. If there is no raise, you can see the flop for "free." Thus the important questions are when to call a raise and when to raise.

You will see many players "protect" their big blinds irrationally — don't be guilty of this. Don't call with Q7 or 84 or other such trash hands. Your blind money is already in the pot — don't vainly chase after it with money you're not *required* to put in. On the other hand, be aware of those players at your table who *will* protect their blinds to extremes. Don't try to steal blinds from those players with a late position raise, but do punish their need to protect hands that should be thrown away.

Raising from the big blind

The more I learn about hold'em, the more I care about position. And when you're in the big blind, your position is awful. So short of the two "big stick" hands (AA and KK) that justify simply pounding your opponents senseless, you need think tactically before raising. Specifically, JJ (and QQ to a lesser extent) are vulnerable to overcards flopping. By raising with them in the big blind[1], you've announced your big hand and created a bigger pot that's hard to abandon, even when the flop is ugly. But there is a very good chance that you will like the flop, and it's best to keep the tactical advantage of secrecy pre-flop.

So I now believe that you are better off not raising with JJ. With QQ, be more inclined to simply check if you can count on one of the late position players to bet for you on a ragged flop. Your plan is often to check-raise a favorable (e.g., jack-high) flop and force out overcards in the middle. And if the flop comes ace-high, most of the time you will check and fold without further investment.[2]

The exception here is when you have very few opponents (and in the big blind you'll know exactly how many you have). With just 1-3 others in the pot, it's less likely that an overcard on the flop will hit somebody, so you can raise with QQ-TT and plan to play aggressively after the flop.

The same tactical concerns hold for hands such as AK and AQ. When playing them from the big blind, your two mostly likely plans on the flop are check-fold and check-raise. The former suggests minimizing your investment before the flop, the latter suggests concealing your plan. So it's best to simply check with these hands. Also note that you're not going to get anybody out of the pot that's already called one bet, so one of the key reasons to raise with those big unsuited aces is now gone.

Interestingly, with the pairs TT on down to 55, you can often raise for value just as you would in late position after a lot of callers. If you have the option to check, look around and see if there are just one or two hands in the muck. If so, it's perfectly fine to raise sometimes with medium pairs.[3] You can also do this with

---

[1]Barry Tanenbaum has dramatically influenced my thinking on this subject. I wish I knew nine years ago what he has taught me since.

[2]We're getting a bit ahead of ourselves discussing post-flop strategy here. But it helps inform your pre-flop actions. Once you've read the chapter about play on the flop, this will make more sense.

[3]The same rule applies: if you don't flop a set, you check and fold on the flop.

hands such as AXs, KQs, and JTs, that give up almost no expected value against large fields.

Defending the big blind against a raise

Quite often you are getting truly huge pot odds — 10:1 or better — when you're in the big blind and there's a single raise. That means that you can play a lot of hands as long as you have cards that can flop a big hand. Any pair, any suited ace, king, or queen, any suited connector or suited one-gap. Avoid unsuited cards unless they're big. Your real danger of defending with something like A7o is that you're up against a better ace, and flopping an ace is only going to cost you money.

If it's two bets cold to you, forget all the above — look for a reason to fold.

Small blind

Depending on how much of a bet the small blind is, you can be fairly liberal in what you play. For instance, in $2-$4 games, the small blind is typically $1 — half a bet. You can call with any reasonable hand: any two suited cards, any connectors down to about 54o, any ace, any king. Still, throw away the trash such as J2 and T4.

If your small blind is only a third of a bet (which is often the case in $3-$6 and $6-$12 games), you need to be tighter. Furthermore, don't forget that you have to act first for the rest of the hand. In rare cases the small blind is two-thirds of a bet.[4] In that case, play just about any two cards (assuming there's no raise, of course).

If there's a raise in front of you, you can largely discount your current investment in the pot. Play it as if you were in middle position and had a raise in front. If your hand could play there, go ahead and call.

Guidelines for raising in the small blind are about the same as in the big blind. The big difference is that you may want to raise or

---

[4]This is actually quite common as you get into higher limit games ($15-$30 and above). In those games, the small blind is almost always 1/2 or 2/3 of a bet.

re-raise to knock the big blind out and isolate yourself against one or two players whom you think you're ahead of (or can out-play after the flop). For instance, if the button is the first person into the pot and raises, you might re-raise with AJo, hoping that he was stealing and you can limit the pot to just the two of you.

Chopping the blinds

Sometimes two players sitting next to each other will agree to "chop" the blinds. That is, if everybody folds in front of them, each will simply take his blind money back and they won't play out the hand.

In general, I recommend against doing this. If you're a better player than your opponents, then you have the edge and should take advantage of it. Also, it gives you practice in the crucially important skill of playing heads-up.

There are, however, two exceptions to that. First, some clubs have a "no flop, no drop" policy in which they don't remove any money from the pot if there's no flop. Many players agree to chop the blinds if such a policy is in effect, and it might be best to go along with it. Second, if you will seriously offend your opponents by refusing to chop, you might want to do it just for your table image. However, most players don't get upset about a player who refuses to chop as long as he's consistent one way or the other.

Free play on the button

In some clubs, the time payment is taken on the button but acts as a blind bet. In those circumstances, you're almost *forced* to play. You have the best position and part or all of a bet in. For instance, suppose the time payment of $2 is taken on the button, but acts as a blind bet in your $3-$6 game. In that case you should call with any two cards. You can call a raise with any hand that would have called a single bet for full price. Since your pot odds are essentially doubled (everybody else is putting in two bets while you're putting in 1.3 bets), you can call a single raise very liberally.

Trash Hands and How to Avoid Them

Texas Hold'em took California by storm in 1987. One of the reasons for its great popularity:

Any two cards can win.

Why, if you had 72, the flop could come all deuces![1]

While many players have learned that playing hands like 72 is a quick way to get rid of your poker bankroll, many have not, or have not learned the lesson very well. Perhaps the most important lesson we can teach you in this book is how to recognize trash hands and get rid of them.

The "dominated" hand

We define a "dominated" hand as one that will virtually *always* lose to another better hand. Even if that better hand does not win, the dominated hand will consistently come in behind.

For instance, consider

---

[1]And it does — about once every 19,600 flops.

If you flop a king with it, you have top pair. However, if you have more than one or two opponents in the pot with you, you run a good chance of being out-kicked (somebody has a king with a better kicker). The only real hope for your hand is a miracle flop like 3-3-x or K-3-x. If the flop comes K-K-x, you probably have the best hand, but nobody is going to call you on that flop unless they can beat you. Time after time you'll get shown KT, KQ, etc.

Furthermore, if even you *do* have the best hand, you can't win much money with it. Suppose you have K3 and flop top pair (i.e., the flop comes king high). If you bet and are called, you dare not bet again, because the caller may well have you beaten. If the caller doesn't have you beaten, he is unlikely to call again. Thus, the best you can do with a dominated hand is win a tiny pot.

Note: in some circumstances we suggest that you can call before the flop with any suited ace, and in some cases, any suited king. However, you're really looking to flop your flush draw (or maybe two pair). If you flop just the ace or king, you have a problem.

Other weak hands

Two-gap and three-gap hands just aren't worth the trouble. Three-gaps are especially bad. For instance, with

you can only make one straight (5-6-7-8-9), and it's not the nuts. If the flop comes nine high, you've got no kicker, and you're vulnerable to overcards.

Small pairs played in the wrong circumstances are bad as well. For instance, with a pair of 4's, you're a tiny statistical favorite over AKs, but where are you going with it? Unless you flop trips, you don't know which card beats you. Your opponent could have AK, AQ, KJ, etc. He could have a small (but larger than your) pocket pair, in which case you're a huge underdog.

Plain trash

There are some hands that you will see played routinely in your low-limit game. You will also occasionally see those hands drag big pots: Hands like 83s, T4o, J6o, 52s, etc. *If you play hands like this regularly, you will lose all your money.* It is that simple.

If you want to play hold'em for entertainment only, and you consider your losses the cost of your entertainment, then go ahead and play trash hands. Otherwise, you must throw them away.

Summary — Trash

Suited faces: QXs, JXs, etc., except where they are specifically mentioned.

Two and three gaps:Q9, Q8, J8, J7, etc., except in very special cases (mentioned elsewhere)

Pseudo-high cards:KX, QX, JX, TX.

Random suited cards:94s, T3s, etc.

Random cards: T2o, 84o, etc.

Deception in Pre-Flop Play

Deception is a fundamental part of poker. You want your opponents to think you're weak when you're strong, and you want them to think you have the nuts when you have nothing. Unfortunately, this goes against what you'd like to do in general: bet and raise with good hands, and minimize your investment in the pot with bad ones.

Deception has varying degrees of importance depending on the poker game you're in. If you're in a big money no-limit hold'em game, deception may play an enormous role. However, in a low-limit hold'em game,

> *You will usually have to show your opponents the best hand to win the pot.*

The two main reasons for this are:

1. In low-limit games, with many players contesting each pot, it's difficult to represent a big hand that you don't have. Either some other player is already looking at that hand, or somebody will call you, almost out of curiosity.

2. Deceiving your opponent requires that your opponent be giving some thought to what you have. Often, your opponent is simply playing *his* cards and hasn't really thought about what *you* have.

For instance, in higher limit games, you can often raise with

before the flop against just one or two players. Then if the flop misses everybody, your bet may win the pot immediately, even against somebody who has flopped bottom pair. However, in a low-limit game, you often have three or four opponents. The probability that the flop missed *everybody* is much lower. Furthermore, the fellow who made bottom pair may decide to call you all the way to the river.

Therefore, deception does not play the role in low-limit hold'em that it does in other games.

Places that deception is useful

Now that we've said all that, we'll discuss where a little deception *is* worthwhile. Just remember that a large percentage of the time you should do the obvious thing.

One deceptive strategy is the "limp-reraise," which is akin to the check-raise after the flop. Since you can't check before the flop, you simply call with a powerful hand and then re-raise when there's a raise behind you. This can be a very powerful play if there's a lot of pre-flop raising going on and you're almost sure that there will be a raise behind you. If you're going to limp-reraise, do it with your biggest hands — huge pairs, AKs, AQs. But you have to do it when you have an almost ironclad guarantee that somebody behind you will raise, allowing you to re-raise. If you're at all unsure, do the raising yourself, and then put in a fourth bet if it's re-raised behind you.

With hands that do better against a lot of opponents (medium pairs, connectors), you can occasionally raise when you know that you have the number of opponents you need. For instance, you can raise with

on the button after a lot of people have called. This mixes up the normal raising that you do with your big pairs and connectors.

Don't waste your big hands

There are two basic versions of deception — playing big hands slowly, and playing small hands fast. Don't waste your big hands by playing them slowly. They are infrequent enough as it is, so when you get one, look for a way to put lots of money in the pot. If you feel the need to be deceptive once in a while, play a small hand (one that can flop big) fast.

The Pre-Flop Raising War

Sometimes an entire table will seem to go on tilt. Pot after pot is capped before the flop. The presence of a couple of maniacs or a player on tilt can be the catalyst for this event.

When this happens, many of the players are doing their gambling before the flop. They'll happily put in four bets with

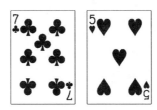

and hope the flop comes 7-7-5 or 3-4-6 or whatever.

In these circumstances, you must hunker down and play very tightly. Throw away hands such as ATo and QJo. You want to play big pocket pairs and big suited connectors — starting hands that can turn into monsters with the right flop. The probability of just top pair getting out of such a hand alive is painfully low — everybody is going to stick around to catch that second pair or inside straight. That said, realize that top pair with a big kicker is how you make your money in hold'em, and this is no exception. Take your chances and take your lumps, but when you have AKs and flop K-7-2, that's *your* flop — play it accordingly.

Understand that raising wars can make your bankroll go through wild swings. You end up paying four or five bets before the flop, and then if the flop hits you the least little bit, you're stuck in there because the pot is so huge.[1] However, winning just one or two of those pots can make you a big winner for the night (or the week).

Remember, when the table gets on tilt, play only your strongest quality hands, and be prepared to go through some rough sailing with them.

---

[1]With all the pre-flop bets in the pot, you are getting correct pot odds to stay for some pretty wild draws such as backdoor flushes and inside straights. This further increases your investment in a long-shot pot.

Quiz on Pre-Flop Play

1. What are the four most important factors to consider when deciding how to play your starting two cards?

2. Define the following terms:
   a) pocket pair
   b) big cards
   c) connectors
   d) one-gap
   e) suited ace

3. Would you prefer to play AKo against two players or seven players?

4. Would you prefer to play 77 against three players or seven players?

5. Define early, middle, and late position.

6. Which pocket pairs can you play in early position, regardless of game conditions? Which pairs can you play if you're in a loose game?

7. Can you play KTo in early position?

8. You are in early position and find yourself holding 98s. Under what circumstances can you play this hand?

9. Under what circumstances can you play a suited ace in middle position?

10. You have 76s in middle position. There is one caller in front of you. The player to your left has raised the last three pots pre-flop. What should you do?

11. You have 54s in middle position. There has been very little raising in your game, and an average of six or seven players taking the flop. Three players call in front of you. What should you do?

12. You are on the button with T8s. Three players call. What do you do? Now consider the same question if the third player raises instead of calls.

13. Suppose you are one in front of the button. Four players have called in front of you. Would you prefer to have KJo or JTs?

14. You have 33 on the big blind. Three players call, and the button raises. What should you do?

15. You have AK on the big blind. Five players call, and nobody raises. What should you do?

16. You have 74s on the button. In this game, the button pays a time charge equal to the big blind, and the time charge plays for you as a bet. There is a raise and two cold calls in front of you. What should you do?

17. You have KK in early position. What percentage of the time best describes how often you would raise (rather than call) with this hand: 90%, 50%, or 10%?

18. You have JTs in middle position. What percentage of the time best describes how often you would raise (rather than call) with this hand: 90%, 50%, or 10%?

19. You have 77 in the "cut-off" position[1] and six players call in front of you. What are reasonable plays?

---

[1]The "cut-off" is the position one in front of the button.

20.   You are in late position with AJo. The last five pots have had the pre-flop betting capped. It's been raised twice before it gets to you. What should you do? Suppose you had AJs instead of AJo. What should you do?

21.   Define a *dominated* hand and give an example.

22.   Under what circumstances would you play Q3o or T5s?

Answers to Quiz on Pre-Flop Play

1. Your cards, your position, the number of players in the pot, and the number of bets required to see the flop.

2. a) pocket pair — two starting cards of the same rank. Examples: QQ, 77.

    b) big cards — two starting cards ten or greater. Examples: AJs, KQo.

    c) connectors — two cards one apart in rank. Examples: T9s, 76.

    d) one-gap — two cards with a single gap in their ranks. Examples: J9s, 86.

    e) suited ace — ace and another card of the same suit. Example: A8s.

3. You would prefer to play AKo against two players. Big cards that are trying to hit top pair with a big kicker or two pair do better against fewer players. You may even win the pot with the "nut no-pair."

4. You would prefer to play 77 against seven players. With only three opponents, you are not getting sufficient pot odds to hit a set, and it's difficult to tell if your unimproved pair is best. However, with seven opponents you are getting the right odds (including implied odds) to flop a set.

5. In a nine-person game, early position is the first four positions to the left of the button. Middle position is the next three positions. Late position is the last two positions, including the button.

6. You can always play AA-77. If the game is loose, you can play any pair.

7. Don't play KTo in early position. Don't even play KJo in early position.

8. If you are in a loose-passive game (many callers, little raising), you can play 98s in early position. If there is a lot of raising going on, even with a lot of players, you should not be playing 98s that early.

9. If you have two or three callers (but no raise) in front of you, and you have little reason to suspect a raise behind you.

10. You have to fold 76s here. There is too good a chance that the person to your left will raise again, and limit the field. You want a lot of players in the pot if you're going to play small suited connectors. Also, you'd rather not pay two bets to see the flop with this hand.

11. In this situation, you can call with 54s. Unlike the situation in the previous question, you are likely to have enough opponents to make your call correct, and you anticipate seeing the flop for only one bet.

12. If there are three callers and no raise in front of you, T8s is an easy call on the button. If the third player raises instead of calling, you should fold T8s.

13. If there are four callers in front, you would rather have JTs, which is a drawing hand and plays better against a large number of opponents. If there were only one caller, you'd much rather have KJo.

14. Assuming the other players call, you will be getting 9:1 to call here. You are less than an 8:1 underdog to flop your set — you can call without hesitation.

15. Raise. This is a different answer from the first edition, but you almost definitely have the best hand, and your raise pounds on players who limped in with bad hands. Realize that the flop may change everything, but you've put more money in the pot with the best hand, and that's the way to win at poker.

16. This is worth a call. You have perfect position, and what looks like a ragged flop could hit you very hard.

17. Raise with the kings at least 90% of the time. An alternative way to vary your play is to pick one specific combination (such as "the red kings") and smooth call with those. That would have you raising with them 83% of the time. If there's a raise behind you, re-raise *every* time.

18. With this drawing hand you don't want to chase players out. Don't raise with this hand more than about 10% of the time.

19. Calling with 77 is perfectly reasonable. But raising might get you the button, costs you nothing in expected value (with that many people in the pot), and might cause your opponents to question your raising standards, which is a good thing. I would raise at least 50% of the time here.

20. Fold AJo here without a second thought. If you had AJs, the call would be much less questionable. However, you're probably going to have to make a flush or two pair to win the pot.

21. A dominated hand is one that is often beaten by better cards, even when it appears to hit the flop. That is, the "good" hand you most frequently make with it often runs into a better hand. Examples: K3 (if you flop top pair you have no kicker), and A6 (same problem).

22. When you can see the flop for *free* (you're in the big blind or have posted) or almost free (e.g., a little blind that's most of a bet).

Introduction to Play on the Flop

The flop is the most crucial juncture of the hand.

Before the flop, you will be playing high quality hands. Your opponents, however, will often be playing all kinds of hands: good, mediocre, and bad. Unfortunately, the value of hands can change dramatically on the flop. Suppose you have

and your opponent has

Let's look at the various odds:

Before the flop: You are a 2:1 favorite

Flop is Q♦-9♥-2♣:You are a 3:1 favorite

Flop is Q♦-8♥-2♣:He is a 3.2:1 favorite

Flop is Q♦-8♠-2♣:He is a 2.5:1 favorite[1]

Flop is Q♠-8♠-2♣:You are even money (1:1)

Flop is A♦-6♥-2♥:You are a 15:1 favorite

Flop is A♦-8♥-2♣:You are a 4:1 favorite

---

[1]Note how much your chances improve just by getting one card toward your flush.

Flop is Q♦-8♥-7♣:He is a 19:1 favorite

Flop is A♦-K♣-2♥:You are a 164:1 favorite

Note two important points here. First, even though AKs is a much better hand than 87o, if the 87o gets help on the flop and the AKs doesn't, the previously weaker hand is now a substantial favorite. The second point is that in all other scenarios, you are a big (or almost unbeatable) favorite. Thus we see that the flop creates a sharp distinction between the favorite and the underdog.

As we discussed in previous chapters, many players will stay after the flop, even when they are huge underdogs. For instance, if the flop comes

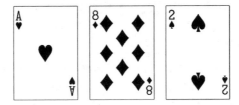

some of your opponents will call a bet (or even two) with 87, hoping to catch another eight or a seven.

On the other hand, you have to realize that your good hands can suddenly become poor ones on the flop. For instance, suppose you have four opponents and the flop is Q♦-9♥-8♥. Your A♠-K♠, which was probably the best hand before the flop, is now almost worthless and should be abandoned if there's a bet.

You want to recognize *on the flop* whether you are the favorite or the underdog, and play (or fold) accordingly. If you call a bet or raise when you don't have the best hand or a good draw,[2] you are giving away money. Conversely, when you have the best hand, you want to maximize the amount of money that goes into the pot. This causes your opponents to make the biggest possible mistakes when they call your bets and raises. As we said at the

---

[2]By "good" draw, we mean one that is correct given the pot odds (or implied odds). For instance, an inside straight draw to the nuts is a good draw only when the pot is fairly large.

beginning of the book, you make most of your money in low-limit games by capitalizing on your opponents' serious mistakes. Unfortunately, there is a problem. Because the pots in low-limit games are often huge before the flop, your opponents may be correct in calling bets on the flop because of the enormous pot odds they're getting. In the next chapter, we discuss how to deal with that problem — how to coerce your opponents into making big mistakes.

Using the flop to get information

The flop is also a good time to probe for information. In structured-limit games, bets and raises are cheaper here than they are on the next two rounds. You can often risk a small bet on the flop that will enable you to make the correct decision later in the hand when more money is at stake.

For instance, suppose you have a pair of pocket kings and raise before the flop, limiting the pot to you and two other players. Alas, the flop has an ace in it. In this situation, bet immediately on the flop. Depending on the response your bet gets, you have an idea of how to proceed.[3] If you check, you show weakness and your opponents will probably bet at you on the turn. This puts you into an unpleasant guessing situation. An assertive bet on the flop might well have prevented the opposing bet on the turn, and told you what you needed to know.

---

[3]And we'll cover how to handle this situation shortly.

The Importance of the Check-Raise

A check-raise is simply checking and then raising when there is a bet behind you. We cannot overstate its importance in low-limit hold'em games.[1]

Why is it so important?

The pot will often be quite large on the flop because there are many callers pre-flop. Furthermore, these players *want* to call your bets on the flop — they did not come down to the card club to fold! Assuming you have the best hand, you now have two possible scenarios:

1. If you have an *excellent* hand — one that is unlikely to be beaten, regardless of the turn and river cards — you are happy to have all these people calling your bets and raises.

2. If you have a *good* hand — one that is probably best right now, but susceptible to being beaten — you would like to eliminate as many opponents as possible. This, of course, is the much more common scenario.

The combination of a large pot and people's desire to call puts you in a bad situation when you have a good, but beatable, hand. Your opponents' instinct (which is to call a lot) *coincides with*

---

[1]You will occasionally hear people say that check-raising (also known as "sandbagging") is improper or unethical poker. This is absurd. Without it, the positional advantage in hold'em (and some other games) is overwhelming. Cheating and unethical poker playing are despicable; check-raising is neither.

correct play. That is, it may be correct for them to call your bet because the pot is large, but they are calling in part simply because they want to call.

Suppose, however, we make your opponents pay two bets rather than one to continue playing. Now, even with a relatively large pot, they may be making a serious mathematical mistake by calling. As we said in the introduction, this is how you make your money at low-limit hold'em.

A classic example

You are on the big blind with

There are three callers, and then a raise in late position. You (correctly) call the raise. Now the flop comes

Usually, you have the best hand here. Of the hands that your opponent was likely to raise with, only AA, KK, and QQ are ahead of you now. Many other good hands (e.g., JJ, TT, AK) are now substantially behind. However, if you bet out immediately, you will be putting the *11th* bet into the pot, making it correct for hands such as 98 and 65 to call. Now suppose you check, and it's checked to the pre-flop raiser. When he bets, you raise; the players in the middle have to call two bets cold. Instead of getting 11:1 pot odds, the player directly behind you is getting only 13:2. If he has 98 or 65, he may decide to fold rather than call two bets. If he chooses to call, *you make money* because the pot odds do not justify his call.

Gaining information

Sometimes you'll check with the intent of check-raising, but things will not turn out as you expect. For instance, the player immediately to your left bets. This is somewhat surprising since many low-limit players are unwilling to bet into a pre-flop raiser (or are waiting to spring a check-raise themselves). Now if the player who raised before the flop raises again, you have learned important information. That is, there are two players who like their hands. It is too early for you to fold, but you will play the hand a bit more gingerly.

Another advantage — the free card

You will find that your opponents in low-limit hold'em will not be as observant as those in higher limit games. However, most people remember being check-raised. If you use the check-raise often on the flop, some of your opponents will become hesitant to bet into you for fear of being check-raised. This can be a significant advantage for you, as in the following example. You call in middle position with

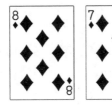

and the flop comes

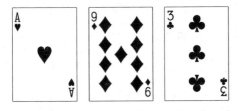

Everybody, including you, checks to the player on the button. If he bets, you can't call because you didn't get any of the flop. However, perhaps he remembers your check-raising him twice during this session, so he checks his A5, and the turn comes

Now you are happy to call a bet on the turn as you have picked up an open-end straight flush draw! Admittedly, this is an exceptional case (you caught the best card you could have hoped for), but it's usually advantageous to get a free card with a hand that couldn't call a bet. In this case, the specter of your check-raising got you the free card.

The problem with the check-raise

When you decide to check-raise, you must be fairly sure that somebody behind you will bet. If you check with the intent of raising but nobody bets, a terrible thing has happened: you have *given* a free card. This is another reason why you have to watch and study your opponents. In the first example above, you would really like to check-raise. However, if the alternatives are betting out immediately or having it checked around the table, then you should of course bet.

Sometimes the reputation that you get for check-raising works to your disadvantage — people are unwilling to bet for fear that you will check-raise! This is good when you have a bad hand with which you'd like to get a free card. It's bad when you have a good hand and want to check-raise. Since you could use a free card more often than you have a check-raising hand, it's okay that your opponents are intimidated. However, if your check-raise is to work, you must be confident that at least one of your opponents is prepared to bet.

Note: in a very small number of public cardrooms and casinos, check-raising is not permitted. It is also prohibited in some home games. If so, your only potent weapon to use up front is gone. You must play *extremely* tightly in front, and bet all your good hands immediately. Hold'em without the check-raise is a crippled game.

Playing When You Flop a Pair

This is how you make your money in hold'em: you have top pair with the best kicker. In fact, against just one or two opponents, you should take top pair (with the best or second best kicker) to a showdown virtually every time.

When you flop top pair with a good kicker

This is generally a very good flop for you. Suppose you have raised with

in late position, four other players have called, and there has been no other raise. The flop comes

You probably have the best hand right now. However, there are a lot of things than can go wrong. If the turn card is

you have to fold if there's any substantial action. Therefore, you want to bet (or raise) immediately on the flop, and make it expensive for overcards to stick around. Even if the board is less threatening (for instance, J♦-6♥-3♣), you still want to raise on the flop. This may get out hands like KQ, which you would like to do. If it's checked to you, bet.

If you're in early position and you get the first flop, you have a problem. You would like to check-raise, but you must be *very* sure that somebody will bet. You definitely don't want to give a free card to somebody with KQ or two hearts. If somebody in late position raised before the flop, he may well bet on the flop, giving you the opportunity to check-raise.

If you were the pre-flop raiser, be more inclined to bet (rather than check-raise) on the flop if the flop hits you. Being the pre-flop raiser, you're almost expected to bet, and this gives you the chance to re-raise if somebody raises behind you.

Note that if you have K♣–Q♦ and the flop comes K♦-8♥-3♣, the check-raise is an excellent play because you aren't afraid of an overcard (except an ace) on the turn. If it's checked around, that's unfortunate, but not likely to be catastrophic. It may also confuse your opponents when you bet on the turn. For instance, if the turn is the T♦, somebody with a ten may call you both on the turn and the river, not believing you have the king.

Let's return to the situation where you have A♣-J♣ and the flop is J♦-9♥-2♥. If you raise and are re-raised (or bet and are raised), you must decide how to continue. If you think that raising again will limit the pot to you and the raiser, it may be worth re-raising, even if he might have a better hand.[1] By eliminating the other players, you are giving yourself a better shot to win the pot (even though it will cost you an extra bet here). For instance, many players would stay in here with a hand like Q♥-9♦. For one bet, that would not be a terrible play. However, if you re-raise and force that person to call two bets cold, he will probably fold. By knocking him out, you save the pot for yourself if a queen, nine, or two more hearts fall.

If you don't think you can eliminate other players or you are sure that the raiser has a strong hand, you can back off — call the raise and then check and call to the river. If you are playing this pot heads-up, it will be almost impossible to fold in this situation even if a third flush card, king, or queen hits. If one of those scary cards comes and there is a lot of raising among multiple players, then you can consider folding. However, if you call a bet on the turn, you must be absolutely sure of your opponent if you decide to fold on the river. By that time, the pot will be quite large, and you will be making a *catastrophic* mistake if you fold incorrectly. We are not urging you to call *every* bet on the river. Nevertheless, an incorrect fold in this situation can be very expensive, depending on how badly you mis-estimate the odds that you are beaten versus the pot odds.

When you flop top pair with a medium/bad kicker

The most common way this can happen is when you have AXs, hoping to get a flush draw, and just an ace flops. For instance, you have

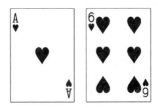

---

[1]It is unlikely that he has you beaten unless his pre-flop play suggested a monster pair. You have the top pair with an ace kicker and there are a number of draws (e.g., QT, two hearts) that he could be playing aggressively.

in the cut-off position. Five people call in front of you, you call, and then the button calls. Now the flop comes

You have flopped top pair, but you can't like it very much. You have six opponents, and if any of them has an ace, you are probably out-kicked.[2] Furthermore, there is no obvious draw that your opponents can have, so if they stick around, it's more likely because they have a better hand than you. In a situation like this, if there is much action, you have to get out. Sometimes when you get out, you will later discover that you had the best hand on the flop, but there is no shame in occasionally folding the best hand. If there is a bet and raise in front of you, you can drop right there and save yourself further anguish. Even if there is a bet and a lot of callers, you should still fold.

If there is a bet and you are first to act after the bettor (players between you folded or the bettor is on your immediate right), you want to raise. This is a positional raise designed to give you control of the hand. On your best days, everybody but the original bettor will fold, and he will check to you on the turn. Your play at this point is based on whether you think your opponent has an ace (quite possibly with a better kicker) or a draw. If the texture of the board (and your knowledge of his play) suggests that he is on a flush or straight draw, tend to bet the turn. If there are no obvious draws on the board, consider checking the turn (i.e., taking a free card). If you check the turn, you almost have to call a bet on the river.

Note that we did not recommend *calling* in this situation. This is an excellent example of tight-aggressive play. Either get out, or

---

[2]Note that if somebody has A9, you're drawing almost dead. That is, since your opponent already has two pair and his lower pair is higher than your kicker, you need two running sixes to win the pot.

use your position to get a free card if you think you need one. There is one exception to this. If the bettor is a maniac or a habitual bluffer (and you're heads-up with him), you do better to simply call all the way. If he is bluffing, you will win more money by letting him continue to believe his bluff might work. If he has a better hand, then you lose less by not raising.

If you are in late position and it's checked to you, go ahead and bet, but hope that all your opponents fold. If not, reassess the situation on the turn. If lots of people call on the flop and/or you can't figure out what they could be drawing to, then be inclined to check the turn. If you thin the field substantially with your flop bet and you believe you are up against drawing hands, tend to bet.

If you are in early position with such a hand,[3] you have to check and fold if there is significant action behind you. You have no position to use, and you cannot be the least bit sure you have the best hand. If everybody checks on the flop and the turn is not threatening, go ahead and bet, hoping to win the pot right there.

If at any point during any of these scenarios you are raised on the turn, and *particularly* if you are check-raised, you should almost always fold (note that it will cost you two more big bets to get to the showdown now).

This whole discussion points out perfectly our concept of the dominated hand. You will be sorely tempted to call bets (and raises) all the way to the river with your top-pair-no-kicker hand, and yet time after time you will get shown a pair of aces with a better kicker. In the long run, *especially* against many opponents, you will come out ahead by dropping that hand as soon as it

---

[3]We hope you had a free play in the big blind.

misses its flush draw. Note that if you get one of your flush cards on the flop, you are in a different situation. Suppose you have

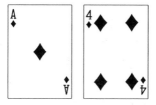

and call on the button after four others have called. If the flop is

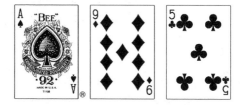

you should call a bet on the flop. If the turn is a diamond, you have picked up the nut flush draw, and can easily call a bet. If you do not pick up your flush draw (or otherwise improve) on the turn, you are back to the earlier situation and have to drop.

An alternative in the above situation is to raise on the flop, and then plan to check the turn. Once you've done that, you will need to call a bet on the river, as your check on the turn may well induce somebody to bet.

You can see that handling top pair with a questionable kicker gets quite messy. There is a way to avoid this mess, and it should always inform your behavior in these situations:

If you think you have kicker trouble, get out of the hand.

When you flop second or bottom pair

Normally, it's best to check and fold when you flop second pair.

Let's consider the exceptions. The first requirement is that the pot be large, but in low-limit games that is often true. To continue playing you must also have an overcard kicker (your unpaired card is higher than any card on the board) and/or backdoor draws. For example, suppose you have A♠-T♠, and the flop comes K♥-T♣-4♠. You have second pair, with an overcard kicker, and three to the nut flush. If the pot is big, you can call a bet on the flop, hoping to catch an ace, ten, or spade on the turn.

Note that you should *not* call a bet with T♠-9♠ if the flop is K♥-T♣-4♦. Now you have neither an overcard nor a backdoor shot at a flush. If the 4♦ was the 4♠, giving you three to your flush, you are about a 3.4:1 dog to somebody with AK, but some of your outs involve drawing again on the turn. Given that you may make your two pair or flush and still get beaten, you should be getting at least 12:1 odds to call in this situation.

The answer is even more clear-cut if you flop only bottom pair. Unless the pot is huge, and you have the secondary outs described above, save your money and fold.

Pocket Pairs on the Flop

Hold'em players are notorious for their inability to abandon pocket pairs, even when the flop demands otherwise. You routinely see players call on the river with a pocket pair that has ended up being the third or fourth best pair within the board: "I had to call — I had a pocket pair." No, you don't have to call. A pocket pair is just a pair until and unless it develops otherwise. But since they are a bit different from pairs that you make with the board, we'll give them their own chapter.

When your pocket pair doesn't improve

If you have a pocket pair that is an overpair on the flop, you have an excellent hand. You can beat top pair with *any* kicker. Treat this as you would top pair on the flop, but you can be even more aggressive.

For example, suppose you have Q♥-Q♦ and the flop comes J♣-7♣-2♥. Now if you bet and are raised, you should make it three bets. You can beat AJ or KJ (which most people would raise with), and you are about 2:1 ahead of a club flush draw. There are two good alternatives to re-raising. One is to call the raise and then check-raise the turn. This way you collect extra by getting a raise on the turn, when the bets are larger. Use this strategy against overly aggressive opponents and those who are likely to overvalue second-best hands such as JT. The other alternative is to call the raise on the flop and then come out betting on the turn. This "stop-and-go" play has become quite popular as a middle ground between a passive "check-and-call" and potentially over-aggressive re-raising out of position. Use this tactic when you aren't quite as confident that you have the best hand (perhaps *you* have KJ), but want to get at least one bet in on the turn.

You have the same problem deciding whether to bet out or check-raise when you have flopped an overpair. This is not the same as when you have AJ and the flop comes jack high; in that case you are afraid of a king or a queen falling. If you have pocket jacks, and the flop comes nine high, you are afraid of a king, queen, *or* ace. Now you must be that much more sure that somebody will bet if you want to check-raise.

Note that if you attempt a check-raise, your intent is to knock out players between you and the bettor by forcing them to call two bets cold. If you don't expect that to work, come out betting.

If your pocket pair is *not* the top pair after the flop, drop it. You are a 23:1 dog to make your set on the turn, so the pot odds (or implied odds) must be that high if you don't have the best hand or other draws. This is not impossible, but it is rare — even in loose low-limit games. Also realize that the betting that made the pot so big may indicate that you're drawing dead. For instance, suppose you have QQ, five players put four bets each into the pot before the flop, and the flop comes ace high. There's a chance somebody has flopped a set of aces, and turning your third queen is only going to cost you a lot of money.

Big pocket pairs and overcards

One of the most frustrating situations in hold'em is starting off with a monster hand, and then getting a flop that spells serious trouble for it. The classic case is, of course, you raising (or re-raising or re-re-raising) with pocket kings and then seeing an ace (but no king) on the flop. Now if anybody holds an ace, you are drawing at two elusive outs. But if not, you're probably way in front. What to do?

If you have five or more opponents, don't even bet. Somebody has an ace. It might be A6o and he had no business calling your raise. It doesn't matter; he has you badly beaten. Check and quietly fold. Don't whine, don't show (or even tell) anybody what you're doing. Abandon your kings and await your next hand.

If you have just one or two opponents, then one of them is going to have to show you an ace. Your plan should be to get to the showdown cheaply. For instance, if you have position, raise the flop, then check the turn, and plan to call a bet on the river.

If the number of opponents is somewhere in between (3-4), then you have to use your judgment in deciding how far to go. Play the flop aggressively and see if you can narrow the field. On the turn, count opponents again and ask yourself if you can realistically put them on draws. Again, be less inclined to pursue the hand if there are many opponents and/or there are no credible draws on the board.

Playing When You Flop Two Pair

Note that initially we are discussing a *split* two pair — when you have two different ranks in your hand, and you flop one of each of them. We will discuss the "pair on the board" situation later in this chapter.

Two pair is a powerful hand that you can play quite strongly. However, it is rarely strong enough to slow play. If you are playing quality hands, your two cards will be close to each other in rank (AXs being the obvious exception). That means that if you flop two pair you have to worry about a straight draw, if not a made straight. Adding the possibility of a flush draw, you have a hand that demands to be played fast; you need to reduce the odds for drawing hands.

When you flop top two pair

Suppose you have

and the flop comes

You can be almost certain that you have the best hand right now.[1] However, you are susceptible to lots of draws. You are essentially even money with somebody who has

Remember also that in low-limit games, the pot is often already big. You should do whatever you think will get the most money in the pot on the flop. If you think that a player behind you will raise, bet out immediately and hope you get to re-raise. If you think somebody will bet but not raise, check-raise. Of course, this is a situation where you don't want to give a free card, so if there's any doubt in your mind, bet.

If somebody puts in a third or fourth raise on the flop, you need to consider the possibility that he has a set. Now it might be correct to check and call on the turn and river. If you put in the last raise on the flop, you can bet this hand all the way to the end if the board is not threatening. For instance, suppose the final board is J♣-T♥-5♥-8♦-7♥. You should definitely bet when the 8♦ hits on the turn, but the 7♥ on the river is a terrifying card, as any nine makes a straight, and a flush is possible. You should check, and call if there is no raise. If there's a raise, you'd have to fold here.

Even if the flop is J♣-T♥-7♥ (which makes a straight possible), you should play this hand aggressively. Top two pair is a very

---

[1]If you don't, there's not much to do. You will lose some money with this hand if it gets beaten, but far more often you will win money with it.

strong hand; don't let the fear of monsters under the bed slow you down.

Flop texture

Flop "texture" is the relationship of the cards on the flop to each other. Are they close in rank or far apart? Are there two (or three) cards of the same suit?

You might be wondering why a subsection on flop texture appears in the middle of a discussion about flopping two pair. That's because the texture of the flop is always important in how you proceed in a hand, and we've reached a good time to discuss it, since the hands we're about to discuss can range in strength from extremely strong to terrifyingly vulnerable. The difference in that strength is closely correlated to the flop texture.

The question we're trying to answer is: "How vulnerable am I to draws and other cards that will hurt my hand?" The more turn cards you can imagine that will concern you, the more action you should put in on the flop. Two pair is a sufficiently strong hand that you would like to wait until the turn to raise, but if there are a lot of cards that will make you unwilling to raise on the turn then you should raise on the flop.

As an example, suppose you have

And the flop comes

If another queen hits, you have just about nothing — note that any queen or even 87 beats you. Also, there are straight draws such as T9, 87, and 54 to worry about. Therefore, it's all the more important that you get your bets in on the flop. Also, don't be so eager to re-raise a second or third time as you would with top two pair. In the situation above, you'd like to believe that nobody was playing Q7, but in loose low-limit games, your opponents will routinely show you that (and Q6, too).

Here's another example. You're on the button with KTs, and the flop comes K-J-T rainbow. Any ace, queen, or nine on the turn will terrify you, and a jack counterfeits your hand. Again, get your raises in on the flop. If the turn is one of the scary cards, you'll have to slow down significantly. Otherwise, keep betting.

This KTs example emphasizes an important point: as a good hold'em player, most of the cards you play are close in rank. So if you flop two pair, then straight draws are possible, if not likely. If you flop "top and bottom" pairs, then all three cards of the flop are within a small range; big straight draws are almost a certainty.

Let's consider one example where there are no apparent draws. You have called one bet on the button with A4s, planning to flop a flush draw. But you accidentally flop two pair with a flop of A-9-4 rainbow. Note that while there are *possible* gutshot straight draws,[2] this is a safe enough flop that you can wait until the turn to put in a raise. When the turn comes, it is likely to create more draws (perhaps adding a backdoor flush draw). By waiting to raise, you will force your opponents to call two big bets with only one card to come. You are charging more for the draws when you are a bigger favorite. This AXs example is the only situation when you flop top and bottom pair and can wait until the turn to raise.

Another important aspect of this flop is that it contains an ace. Many hold'em players are almost unable to fold a hand contain-

---

[2] An interesting bit of trivia: any flop containing an ace can make *some* straight possible on the turn.

ing an ace. And so you can be more certain that an opponent is holding top pair and that another bet will be coming on the turn; you'll have the chance to raise.

Waiting to unleash the raise

It is worth summarizing the rules for when you can wait until the turn to put in your raise (and this applies to one-pair hands as well):

1. You are relatively unconcerned about possible draws arriving on the turn. As a rule of thumb, if there's a flush draw possible, raise on the flop. If there's more than one open-end straight draw that could be held by connectors (e.g., QJ, 87), raise on the flop. Of course, the more opponents you have, the less you should be inclined to wait to raise.

2. You have to believe that you can get in a *raise* on the turn. Is your opponent likely to still believe he has the best hand on the turn? For instance, if you think he's betting top pair, then it's better if that top pair is an ace than a queen. If it's a queen, then an ace or king on the turn may cause him to check. Of course, if your opponent is hyper-aggressive, then there's a good chance he'll bet the turn anyway.

Being out of position

I covered the whole discussion of flop texture with the assumption that you have position on your opponent(s) and are last to act (or close to it). It's reasonable to do this because you'll be playing many more hands when you have good position. So statistically, more of your post-flop poker is played from good position. But you need to understand what to do when you're out of position:

Play more directly when you're out of position.

It's that simple. For instance, remember that one of our rules for waiting until the turn to raise was that you had to be relatively sure you could get in a raise. If you're in position and your opponent spoils your plan by checking, at least you get in a bet. If he spoils it by checking when you were planning a check-raise, then you don't collect *any* big bets on the turn. So if you need a check-raise, get it in on the flop, and then bet the turn.

Two pair with a pair on the board

This situation is far less desirable than a split two pair. For instance, you have raised with

and the flop comes

Unfortunately, in low-limit games, many players are willing to play almost *any* two cards, so it's hard to figure the probability of somebody having an eight. There is one obvious consideration — the more opponents you have, the more likely it is that one of them has flopped trips.

In this particular case, there are a lot of draws possible. J9 and 97 both make open end straight draws,[3] and there is a heart flush draw possible. Therefore, you are ahead of many hands that people will play beyond the flop. This forces you to play more assertively to avoid giving free cards.[4]

---

[3]Of course, you're delighted if J9 hits the top end of his straight with a queen, as that gives you a full house.

[4]This is a change in my thinking from the first two editions, where I advocated being ready to abandon the hand in this case. I am now persuaded that with all these draws possible, you can't give up until given a stronger sign that things are not going your way.

Bet or raise on the flop, and then plan to bet the turn too. You would like to get any ace or king to fold here, and they are not getting the right price to call. If you get raised on the turn, *then* it may be time to get out. This is particularly true if you get check-raised (a check-raise tends to speak more strongly about a player's hand than a simple raise). You have to take the mindset of the raiser into consideration, but if you're check-raised by a rational player on the turn, dump the queens.

If a heart comes on the turn and you still have multiple opponents (perhaps three or more), then you may need to get out if there's lots of action. There are too many ways you can be beaten.

Note that the situation is somewhat different if the flop is J-5-5 of three different suits and you have KK. Now you're not as afraid of overcards on the river, and there's no draw you can imagine your opponents having. In this case, it may be correct to check the turn, and then call a bet on the river (or bet if they check to you again). Your decision here should be based on how many people call after you bet (or raise) the flop. *Be especially leery of a reasonable player who calls two bets cold on the flop.* If just one or two players call, then you can reasonably put them on jacks or overcards and continue betting. If you look around on the turn and see a lot of people with cards, checking is the best choice. Again, if you bet and are check-raised by a reasonable player, you need to fold without calling the raise *most* of the time. Only call once in a while to prevent sharp opponents from check-raising you to death on the turn.

This situation (the J-5-5 rainbow flop with you holding kings) is known in the poker community as, "way in front or way behind." That is, one of you is probably dramatically ahead of the other; it's just not clear who is in front. If your opponent has JT, then he has only two outs.[5] Conversely, if he does have one of the dreaded fives, then *you* have only two outs. When you are way in front or way behind, checking is a fine play.

---

[5]Note that hitting a ten does him no good since your kings and fives would beat his jacks and tens.

Your plan should be similar if you flop top pair along with a paired board. As an example, you have A♦-J♣ and the flop comes J♠-6♥-6♦. There are no draws imaginable, so it's scarier when people call your bet on the flop.

Big pair with a paired overcard

Suppose you raise with QQ. Would you rather see the flop K-7-2 or K-K-7? Of course, you'd rather see nothing bigger than a queen at all, but between these two flops, the latter is much preferable. First, it actually makes it less likely that any of your opponents holds a king. Second, it means that somebody with something like 87 can't hit a second pair to beat you. The pair of kings on the board "counterfeits" any split two pair that somebody makes.

In a situation like this, you should bet. Anybody holding a king is likely to slow play,[6] and you want to decloak them at least to the extent that they're forced to call a bet. If you have more than one or two opponents on the turn, then you should check and fold — one of them (at least) has a king. Against one or two opponents, you treat your queens as the best hand and should bet the turn. If you get raised on the turn, then you're almost certainly looking at a king and can fold.

A bluffing opportunity

Note that the situation is not hopeless. In a nine-person game, if you see two eights on the flop and you don't have one, there is a 40% chance that nobody at the table was dealt an eight. Furthermore, somebody may have folded an eight (watch for signs that somebody is upset about dropping before the flop). This is one of the few situations in a low-limit game where you can try a pure bluff. If nobody has an eight, you might win the pot right there with a bet, even if you have nothing.

---

[6]Though this is a mistake.

Playing When You Flop Trips

Low-limit hold'em players lose a lot of money by not playing trips fast enough.

You flop trips very infrequently: about 11% of the time when you hold a pocket pair, and less than 2% of the time when you hold two cards of different rank. However, you will often make a lot of money when you get these hands.

When you flop a set

A "set" is three of a kind when you have two of the rank in your hand and a third one is on the board. This is an extremely powerful hand (partially because it is so well hidden), and many players are tempted to play it slowly so they can extract the most money from their opponents. This brings us to the sentence at the beginning of the chapter: almost all the time, you do better by playing your set fast, putting in as many bets and raises as possible. This is particularly true in low-limit hold'em because you will not scare players out of the pot the way you would in higher limit games. For instance, if you get somebody opposite you at the table with two pair, you will often cap the betting between you, making it terribly expensive for straight and flush draws. In low-limit games, you may trap in players who have only two overcards and are drawing dead.

However, if you play the hand slowly, you are giving hands such as inside straight draws a better chance to beat you. For instance, suppose you have

And the flop comes

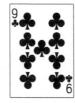  

You have flopped the absolute nuts. However, if a club or any 3, 5, 6, 8, T, or J comes on the turn, you may no longer be in front (you are a 3.4:1 dog to make a full house or quads on the river). Thus, in most cases, you want to get lots of money in the pot right now. You are an almost 3:1 favorite over an open-end straight draw, and you will still win 58% of the pots against *both* an open-end straight draw and a club flush draw in this situation. When your opponents put money in the pot, you are getting an enormous return on your investment.

Conversely, if you let them in cheaply, they are getting much better odds on their draws, making those draws either less of a mistake, or even correct. If that is the case, you are losing money. For instance, if there is a bet in front of you and you flat call, a player with

is getting correct implied odds to call (trying to catch an eight) if there were about six bets in the pot before the flop. However, if you raise the original bettor, a person who calls with an inside straight draw (even to the nuts) is making a mistake. That's because he really only has four outs (the eights) though he probably believes he has ten (the eights, three jacks, and three tens).

Often you will hear players say, "There was no point in betting (or raising) — he would have called with his flush draw anyway." The latter half of this statement is true, but misleading. A player who calls your bets or raises when he has flopped four to a flush is not making a mistake. However, if you check and let him draw at his flush for free, you are giving him *infinite* odds on his draw (pot size: 0), which is far better for him than your charging him a bet for his draw. The situation is similar, but not quite as bad, if you call a bet rather than raising.

Note that typically you are *both* doing the correct thing. If there are players in the pot other than you and the flush draw, they are subsidizing both of you. Since you have the best hand, you have the most equity in the pot and benefit from every dollar that goes in. Your opponent with the flush draw is getting the correct pot odds (2:1) to draw. Everybody else is making a serious mistake, as it's likely they're drawing dead or near-dead.

Remember, if you raise on the flop with your set, and half as many people call as would have called a single bet, you have gotten the same amount of money in the pot but you're competing with half as many opponents. Slow playing is intended to let lesser hands catch up to a monster — and your set is not a monster (yet).

Exceptions

There are two cases in which you might want to slow down after you've flopped a set:

1. You are very sure you have the best hand and are willing to risk giving your opponents a cheap card in hopes of building a bigger pot.

2.   You're concerned that you may not have the best hand.

Let's consider the first case. Suppose you have a pair of red sevens, and the flop comes

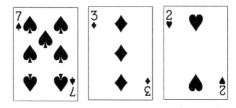

Especially if you are in late position, you may want to just call if there is a bet in front of you, or even check if there hasn't been a bet. You are taking a risk (note that a 4, 5, 6, or ace could give somebody a straight), but it may be worth it. With this flop, you won't get much action from many hands. However, if a card like the 3♠ comes on the turn, maybe you can catch an opponent (or two) with a three, and even get some spade flush draws interested. Of course, you're happy for this to happen because it's virtually impossible for anybody to catch up with you if another three does fall. If something like the 8♦ comes, you may now have a problem because somebody could have picked up a very big draw. However, you can now bet or raise on the turn and make it a questionable play for those draws to stay in.

Note that this is the exceptional case. If the flop contains any two cards of the same suit, you are better off playing fast.

Also, the higher your set, the more you can think about slow playing. If you have raised with pocket aces and the flop comes A-7-2 rainbow, then you can just call any bets or raises. If you're in the pot with 77 and get the same flop, you should raise immediately.

Another case in which you can slow down is when your opponent shows aggression on the flop. Suppose you are in the situation above (you have pocket sevens and flop top set) in early position. You bet out and are raised by a player in late position. You can choose to re-raise on the flop, or wait until the turn. If you go with the latter plan, your intent on the turn should be to trap as many people as possible for as many bets as possible. If most of the players are between you and the raiser, bet out. If he raises, re-raise. If the raiser is immediately behind you, then go for the check-raise, hoping players behind him will call his bet, and then you get to raise them.

Now consider the other case — what if you're afraid you're up against a bigger hand? This is an unusual scenario. However, suppose you have a pair of red nines and get a flop like

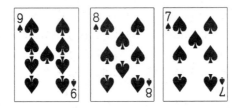

Even now, start out playing fairly fast. There is a chance you're up against a made straight or a flush. There's even a chance you're drawing dead to a straight flush.[1] However, you don't want to give a single ten or spade a free card, so you have to grit your teeth and bet or raise. If you are re-raised, you can back off (call) to see how the turn and river cards look. Note that with a pair of red aces, you would play this hand very fast on the flop, but you'd be prepared to drop them if a lot of players were betting and raising. With a set, you can't get away so easily. You have to see this hand to the end, so you may want to ease up and see what the turn and river cards bring. Now if the board pairs, you *hope* somebody made a straight and somebody else made a flush, because you beat them both and they'll likely call a raise on the river.

If the pot has gotten big on the flop (i.e., there's been a raise or two and/or many players in the hand) don't even think about slow playing; get your raises in immediately.

---

[1] There is also a saying that if you get a set beaten and don't lose a lot of chips, you didn't play it right. This is somewhat simplistic, but emphasizes the importance of playing aggressively with a hand this strong.

A final thought about sets — if you *never* folded after flopping a set, you wouldn't be making much of a mistake. Play them fast, and plan to go to the river with them.

When you flop trips (with a pair on the board)

You have to play this hand much more delicately than you do a flopped set. With a pair on the board, everybody will be nervous about where the other two of that rank are. If another player is aggressive, you may be looking at the fourth card of that rank, a hand that can beat trips, a bluff, or a hand that looks good but isn't as good as yours. Let's consider an example. You have

in late position with four callers in front of you and the flop comes

If somebody bets here, raise. The pot has gotten fairly large (especially if the bettor is early and there are callers in between), and your hand isn't strong enough to slow play. If somebody re-raises you, there's a reasonable chance that he has the last eight. Now you back off and call any bets.

A lot of players will raise with a queen in this situation, but with an eight they will wait to raise on the turn.[2] Therefore, if you bet and somebody raises, it doesn't prove that he has the last eight in

[2]Another reason for you to raise on the flop with a third eight. You're getting more money in the pot, and may actually be persuading your opponents that you *don't* have the eight.

the deck. This is a good time to try for a check-raise on the turn, as your opponent with a queen (or less) may bet the turn. Again, figure out what will trap the most players for the most bets and do that.

If you have a very strong kicker with your trips, you want to play it even faster. In the case above, if you have A♦-8♦ instead of 8♦-7♦, you can put in four or five bets. This severely punishes somebody who has the case eight but no kicker. It also puts the most possible pressure on straight and flush draws. Sometimes the person with the smaller kicker will get lucky and pair his kicker to make a full house — you simply take that chance. If you're pretty sure you have the best kicker with the trips, play the hand very strongly.

In looser hold'em games, you will almost assuredly get to the river with trips. In the above case, only another queen falling would make you inclined to drop. Even then, you would have to be quite sure there was a third queen somewhere because the pot would probably be enormous. Of course, if the board is terribly scary for you (for instance, you have T♠-8♠ and the board is showing 8♦-8♣-7♦-6♣-5♦) and there is a lot of action, save your money and get out. Learning when to fold strong hands takes years of experience and practice. It is one of the skills you must develop to move to higher limits and tougher games.

Playing When You Flop a Straight or Flush Draw

Straight and flush draws are much stronger hands in low-limit games than they are with bigger limits. The main reasons for this are:

1. As we have discussed previously, you will often have many opponents in the pot with you. Their presence makes the straight and flush draws correct in cases that would not be right if you had fewer opponents. In short, you are getting the necessary pot odds.

2. You will get paid off more often when you do make your hand — the pots will be (relatively) bigger than they are in more expensive games, and your opponents are more inclined to call. In short, you are getting better implied odds.

3. Because there are typically so many players in a hand, the average winning hand will be closer to the best *possible* hand (i.e., the nuts) than it is in a tighter game. The best possible hand for any given board is rarely less than a straight, so you will need these more powerful hands more frequently to win a pot.

Since you are drawing, you want many players to stay in the pot with you (just as you do with drawing hands before the flop). In fact, you are often in a situation where you can bet or raise your draws for value. "For value" means that with enough callers, you show a profit on bets you make, even though you're still drawing.

Thus, your goal is to get as many players as possible to put in as many bets as possible.

Flush draws and open-end straight draws

Consider this example.[1] You are in late position with

There are three callers in front of you, you call, the button raises, and everybody calls. Now the flop comes

Note that there are *eleven* bets in the pot already. You would like to get as many people into the pot as you can. You are slightly less than a 2:1 underdog to make your flush, so you are making money if you can get at least three other people in the pot with you. You need to get slightly better than the exact odds since you could make the flush but have it beaten by a full house.

You would like to bet, but the problem is that if you bet and the button raises, he may force out the early position players; you don't want that. In this case, check and hope the button bets. If you get a lot of callers in front, then you can consider a check-raise. But you don't want the button to re-raise and knock out the other players.

---

[1]For much of this chapter you can consider straight and flush draws interchangeably. A four-flush is a 1.9:1 underdog to make a flush by the river. The open-ended straight draw is a 2.2:1 underdog. These are close enough to consider equivalent for now.

In low-limit games, you will often have three or more opponents with you on the flop. In that case, just try to maximize the number of bets that go in. If three bets are going into the pot for every bet you put in, you are getting much the best of it. Of course, this assumes that you're drawing at the nut flush or straight. If you aren't, you need to consider the possibility that your hand won't be good if you make it. With a draw to less than the nuts, you can still call the bets and raises, but you shouldn't be putting them in yourself unless you have other value, such as a pair.

Raising with a draw in late position can also have the desirable side effect of getting you a "free"[2] card on the turn should you need one. Suppose you have A♠-J♠ on the button and there were three calls in front of you pre-flop. You call, as do both blinds, and the flop comes as above (Q♠-4♠-T♥). You have an extremely strong hand — any king or spade (with the minor exception of the T♠) gives you the nuts. An ace may give you the best hand as well. If there is a bet and a couple of calls, you should raise as much as 90%-95% of the time. You probably don't have the best hand right now — any pair beats you at the moment — but you are getting excellent odds for your draw (you will make either the straight or the flush 45% of the time). Now if you make your hand on the turn, you can bet. If the turn misses you, you check and get a free river card. You may also get people betting into you on the river after you've checked the turn. Of course, if you make your hand on the river, you get to raise them.

Suppose you are in late position, and call with

---

[2]It's really a "half-price" card. You're paying an extra small bet (e.g., $3) to save a big bet (e.g., $6) on the turn. More about this in "Free Cards and the Importance of Position" beginning on page 130.

after three other players have called. Now the flop comes

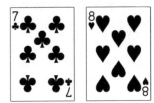 

The first player bets, two people call, and you (correctly) raise with the open-end straight draw. But now the original bettor makes it three bets. If both the original callers stay in, and *particularly* if your cardroom permits only three raises,[3] go ahead and cap it. Since you are getting 3:1 on the bets you put in, you're not taking the worst of it by re-raising. Furthermore, because you've capped the betting in late position, the original bettor doesn't know what you have. For all he can tell, you have pocket eights and are just raising with the best hand. Now there is a very good chance that he'll check to you on the turn.

Note that if the turn is a club, you pick up a flush draw as well. In that case, you may have as many as 15 (or more) outs — you can bet the turn for value against two or more opponents. But even if the turn is of absolutely no use to you, you've accomplished a wonderful thing. That is, you put a bunch of money in the pot on the flop when you were getting good value for your investment, and then not paying a single dime when your odds were slimmer (because you have only one card left to make your straight).

A final benefit of this play: by building a huge pot on the flop, you encourage your opponents to call your bets if you make your hand.

You can also check-raise with a draw if you're sure that people between you and the bettor will call (or if they've already called one bet). Remember, you don't want to shut people out of the hand now. Suppose you are on the big blind with 7♠-6♠. An early position player has raised and gotten two calls. You call as

---

[3] At this writing, every online poker site I'm aware of has a three-raise limit.

well (which is fine). The flop is Q♠-4♥-5♣. You check, the pre-flop raiser bets, and both of the other players call. Raise if you're pretty sure the bettor won't re-raise. Your problem with his re-raising is that he may scare out the callers to his left, and you don't want that. If he just calls, the original callers will call your single raise.

Of course, check-raising in early position puts you in an awkward situation on the turn. If a blank hits, you *have* to check since it's virtually impossible you will win the hand by betting, and you probably won't get the four callers you need to make a bet for value correct (if the turn misses you, you are a 4:1 underdog to make your flush on the river). Your check on the turn shows weakness, and you may be forced to call a bet.

Remember, if you're going to check-raise with a draw, do it with a draw to the nuts.[4]

Double gutshot straight draws

You need to recognize these because they are effectively open-end straight draws made up of two inside straight draws. Suppose you have

---

[4]In his seminal work, *Hold'em Poker*, David Sklansky wrote, "Never check-raise on the flop with a come hand if a pair shows." This is as good advice now as it was when I first read it many years ago, but at the time my ignorance of poker terminology made the sentence almost indecipherable to me.

and the flop comes

If you don't look closely, you may miss the fact that *either* a king or a nine gives you the nuts. Play this hand the way you would an open-end straight draw. In bigger games you'll learn that these hands are especially valuable for their deceptive qualities. At lower-limits, few if any of your opponents will be trying to work the hand backwards to see what you have.

Another example: you have 7♠-5♠ in the big blind, and the flop comes 9♣-6♥-3♠. Any eight or four gives you a straight. However, note that if an eight comes, you don't have the nut straight (check this and be sure you know what *is* the nuts).[5]

Weaker draws

The best draw worth mentioning here is the inside straight draw. Contrary to the advice passed down through innumerable generations of American men ("And son, don't *ever* draw to an inside straight..."), it is often correct in low-limit hold'em to do just that. You are an 11:1 underdog to catch your card on the turn, but you can count on winning two or three big bets if you do (implied odds again). Therefore, you can call a bet on the flop if you're getting about 7:1 odds, assuming that you are drawing at the nuts. For instance, if the flop is two-suited, you must be getting about 10:1 to draw at the inside straight because you might make your straight at the same time somebody makes a flush.

It is even better if you have two overcards to the flop. For instance, suppose you have J♦-T♦ and the flop comes 8♣-7♥-2♠. Now a nine gives you the nuts, and either a jack or ten may give

---

[5]With a board of 9-6-3-8 and no flush possible, T7 makes the nut straight.

you the best hand. This is the best possible situation in which to draw at a "gutshot" straight.

You will occasionally see players drawing at the low (aptly called the "ignorant") end of an inside straight. For example, they have 6♥-5♥, the flop comes 8♣-9♦-A♠, and they call a bet trying to catch a seven. Unless you are getting enormous pot odds — say 20:1 or better — don't do this.

Usually if there's a raise on the flop and you would have to call two bets cold, you are not getting correct odds to draw at an inside straight. If you call a single bet and there's a raise behind you, then you can call. However, you would rather see this situation coming and not call the first bet.

You can sometimes call on the turn with an inside straight draw, but remember you're an 11:1 underdog to make your straight. This is an excellent example of why you need to keep track of the number of bets in the pot — were there 22 small bets in the pot before you had to call on the turn? If so, then you can call with your inside straight draw.[6]

Alert readers of the first two editions will note that I have removed a subsection here that described continuing with two overcards and three to a flush (e.g., you have K♥-Q♥, and the flop comes 8♥-4♦-3♠). Barry Tanenbaum said of this subsection, and I quote, "I hate this. This encourages pointless chases and leaks!" I am persuaded that Barry is correct. Do not call bets in this situation.

Straight draws vs. flush draws

We said at the beginning of this chapter that you could treat straight and flush draws similarly because the odds against your making them were similar. However, there are some differences you need to understand.

---

[6]It is true that you still have some implied odds for bets you'll collect if you make your hand on the river. But implied odds are more powerful on the flop, because if you make your hand on the turn, then you collect both there *and* on the river.

If you flop a straight draw when the flop is two-suited, you must consider the chance that making your straight with the third card of a suit will do you no good. In effect, you have only six outs instead of eight. Even if your straight *is* good when the third of the suit hits, you won't get as much value for it because you can't play as aggressively. Furthermore, opponents you can beat will be less inclined to call because either a straight *or* flush beats them. If a flush draw is possible, you have to be more tactful in handling your straight draw. Continuing this thought, do *not* draw at a straight if there are three of the same suit on the board. You will see other players do it, but throw away a straight draw without a second thought if a flush could be made already. In the long run, this will save you a lot of money.

When the board is paired

You must proceed much more carefully when you flop draws with the board paired — you may be drawing dead, or almost dead. For instance, if you have J♣-T♣ and the flop comes 8♦-8♠-9♥, you have an open-end straight draw. However, if an opponent has 8♥-7♥, your straight draw is actually an inside straight draw because only a queen is good. A seven falling is *terrible* because it makes your straight but gives your opponent a full house.

If you have three or more opponents putting in three or more bets each, get out. Perhaps your draw is live, but it's not worth the trouble. If there is a raise and somebody calls two bets cold, get out — that's often a sign that somebody has flopped a monster. If you can see a turn card for a single bet, then go ahead and do so; do not be putting in the raises yourself.

If the flop is a single suit

If the flop is all one suit, you can continue if you have the nut or second nut flush draw. Anything else, there's too much of a chance that you're drawing dead. Since you may be up against a completed flush already (which reduces your chances of making your flush), don't raise for value — although if you have position, think about raising for a free card and then checking on the turn if you don't make your flush.

Final thought on draws

One of the biggest differences between low-limit hold'em and the bigger games is the number of opportunities to bet draws for value. By doing this correctly, you can win a handful of extra bets during a session and yet be perceived as somebody who "gambles." That is, you don't want your opponents to think you play only quality cards and good draws. If they realize that, they won't pay you off when you make big hands. Putting a lot of bets into the pot with a draw is often viewed as gambling — going against the odds just for the excitement of the draw. However, with enough opponents, you're doing the mathematically correct thing while your opponents see you playing loose and wild. This is an extraordinarily powerful combination.

Playing When You Flop a Complete Hand

Every once in a great while, you will be fortunate enough to flop a "complete" hand — straight or better.

When you flop a straight

This is the weakest of the complete hands, and is vulnerable to the most draws. Therefore, you want to play a flopped straight fast. Consider the following example: you have

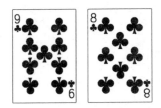

in late position. There are three calls in front of you; the button and both blinds call. Now the flop comes

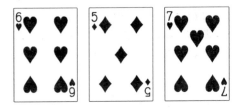

There is a bet and two calls in front of you. Many players would just call in this situation — that's a *mistake* — you should definitely raise. There are already nine bets in the pot, and there are many cards you don't want to see on the turn. If any heart or five through nine falls on the turn, you no longer have the nuts. Furthermore, if somebody has flopped a set or two pair, he may choose to slow play it (which is also a mistake, though in this case it's to his benefit). Your raise may cause him to re-raise immediately and you re-raise again. Note that this puts enormous pressure on heart draws[1] and hands like T♦-8♦, which is important. Of course, playing this fast on the flop will knock out some players who have little or no chance to beat you. You're better off paying that price and forcing draws to pay a premium.

If you flop an ace high straight and there are no flush draws that worry you, you can slow down a little bit. If you have A♠-Q♠ and the flop is K♥-J♦-T♠, it's OK to check and call or just flat call a bet. However, if a lot of action breaks out, you should take off the gloves and start raising yourself — if somebody has two pair or a set, you want to punish them now while you know you have the nuts. By playing slowly, you run the risk of a card such as the Q♣ falling (in which case you have to split the pot with any ace) or a very scary card like the J♥ (which makes full houses possible and may give somebody a heart flush draw). The more players you have against you, the more inclined you should be to play your straight fast.

If you flop the non-nut straight (you have 8♦-7♦ and the flop comes J♠-9♦-T♣), it's even more important to play fast. If an eight, queen, or king comes, you have essentially nothing, so you have to start swinging immediately. Even trying to check-raise is a mistake. Go ahead and bet, hoping you get raised so you can re-raise. If somebody has KQ (or Q8), you are going to lose some chips — you can't give up this hand unless a very scary card hits.

---

[1]Note that A♥–T♥ has about 26% equity in the pot against your nut straight and a set of fives. If it's just the three of you in the pot, the nut flush draw is actually losing a little money on every dollar he puts in. Anybody else in the pot is drawing near dead.

When you flop a flush

This is another situation where many players make a serious mistake by not playing fast enough. If you flop anything but the nut flush, you *must* bet or raise to charge higher flush draws dearly. Suppose you have

in middle position, you call along with four others, the big blind raises, and you all call. Now the flop comes

and the big blind bets out. Slow playing is out of the question here. The pot is so big you'd be happy to win the whole thing right here (but that isn't going to happen). Anybody with the A♦ or K♦ is going to call (which is correct for them). Raise immediately. If somebody makes it three bets, you can flat call, but you still need to bet again on the turn if a blank comes — you don't dare give a single bigger diamond a free card. Again, if somebody has flopped a bigger flush than you, you lose some money. However, far more frequently you have the best hand — but you must play it fast.

If a fourth diamond comes, you are now in a check and call situation, especially if anybody called your raise cold on the flop. There is still some chance you have the best hand, but you don't want to call a raise with it. If a fourth of your suit comes and you have a lower flush (say eight or nine high), you have to give it up. The fact that you most likely were well in front on the flop means nothing — throw your six card flush away if there is significant action.

If you flop the nut flush, you can wait until the turn to raise or check-raise. However, as we discussed with the straight, if a raising war breaks out on the flop, you should start raising as well. If the board pairs, then don't check-raise — you might be giving a full house a chance to make it three big bets. Bet out immediately and hope you are called but not raised. If you are raised, you should call. Only if the board pairs twice should you be willing to abandon the nut flush.

When you flop a full house

With a pocket pair, you will flop a full house a little more than 1% of the time; with two cards of different rank, about 0.1% of the time (one out of a thousand hands). In general, your only concern at this point is how to extract the most money from the hand — your chances of being beaten are minuscule.

With pocket pairs, you can flop a full house in two different ways: one of your rank plus a pair, or trips on the board. Of course, you prefer the former way — in the latter case there's always the danger that somebody has the fourth one.

First, let's consider the "set+pair" scenario. Suppose you have

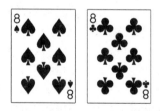

in middle position with six callers. Now the flop comes

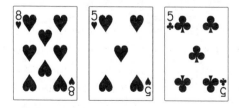

This is an excellent situation for you. Of course, you hope that the other two fives are active[2] and that there is a flush draw around as well. Your hand is altogether strong enough to slow play, but you may not want to do that. If nobody bets, then bet. If somebody bets, just call — don't raise. If you're lucky, the turn will complete the flush, and two other people will do all the raising for you while you are just along for the ride. Things will probably slow down on the river, and that's when you can get in your raise(s).

If no flush or straight draw is possible on the flop, you should slow down a lot, hoping the turn will give some people big draws (that are probably dead). However, once the turn comes, you should start betting and raising. A person with a flush draw will only complete it one out of five times on the river. By raising on the turn, you get these people to call, trying to make their flushes and straights. You're delighted if they make them on the river, but usually they don't, so you need to collect from them on the turn.

The situation is somewhat different if your set is the lower of the two ranks on the board. Suppose you have those same black eights, but the flop is

This is a wonderful flop for you, but not quite as good as the first one. Unlike the first case, there is a small, but important chance you will get out-drawn. Furthermore, you will have to pay off some pretty big raises when you are beaten. However, until "guaranteed" otherwise, you must play this as the best hand. This time, you can't wait to show aggression. Start betting and raising immediately on the flop — with the negligible exceptions of TT or T8, you are winning for now. Don't hesitate to cap the betting on the flop given the opportunity. The same is true on the turn — play the hand strongly. Be willing to put in a third bet on the turn, and only get nervous if somebody puts in a fourth bet. Sometimes you lose to a bigger full house with this hand, but

---

[2]In different hands.

worrying about that very much is seeing monsters under the bed. Play it for the best hand, and just be alert for the small possibility that one of those monsters is real.

If the board pairs (such as two running sixes), you have to fold. Fortunately, this doesn't happen very often, but if you have been getting a lot of action on the turn, and then the turn card pairs, your full house is almost worthless. Furthermore, you're going to get caught in a raising war if both tens are active. Give up and get out.

If the flop is all one rank when you have a pocket pair (.24% of the time), you have an awkward situation. If you have a big pair (tens or higher), you have to stay with it as long as no overcards fall. If an overcard to your pair hits, you are beaten by a single one of those as well as the fourth card of the flopped rank; now you can get out if there's a lot of action. If you have a big pair you should bet the flop to avoid giving bigger cards a free card. Also, in this situation, almost anybody who has flopped the quads is going to slow play. Use bets and raises on the flop to figure out who is willing to stick around. For instance, watch out for a player who calls a raise cold on the flop — proceed carefully. Plan to check and call on the turn and river — somebody with quads will probably wait for big bets to raise.

If you hold two cards of different rank and flop a full house, the situation is similar to flopping top set with a smaller pair. Suppose you hold

and call in middle position after two other callers. Now there is a caller behind you, a raise, and two cold calls. Everybody else calls. The flop comes

You've got the nuts, and the chance of your being out drawn at this point is almost nil. Unfortunately, it's unlikely that you're

going to get much action from anybody. If somebody has the case jack, he'll play with you — other than that you have to hope that there are some straight and flush draws out. You might as well start betting with this hand — hope that the last jack is, in fact, active, and that player starts raising. Many players will stay in with their draws here even though they're drawing dead.

When you flop quads or a straight flush

This happens so infrequently it's hardly worth mentioning. With the quads, you've crippled the deck (i.e., it's unlikely anybody else has a hand that they like much). In a higher limit game, you might want to slow down and relieve the fears of your opponents about who had made trips. In a low-limit game, it doesn't matter much. Check once on the flop to see what people do, but if any betting and raising happens, get in and raise too.

With the straight flush, you want to play fairly fast because if somebody has the ace high flush, he may put in a lot of bets before he figures out he's beaten (assuming the board isn't paired). Your hand is very well hidden and you will get a lot of action from worse hands. Therefore, there's no point in slow playing even though there's (essentially) no danger of your being out drawn.

Summary — Flopping a complete hand

Once again we see that even when you flop a huge hand, you rarely want to slow play it in a low-limit game. Players will not give you credit for the hand that you have and will happily raise even though they may be drawing dead. Give them plenty of opportunities to do this by playing your big hands fast.

Playing When You Flop Two Overcards

Overcards are cards higher than anything on the board. Let's consider an example. You have

and the flop comes

You have two overcards — can you call a bet? Can you bet? Many poker experts say that you can bet or call a bet in this situation. However, it takes a lot of experience and knowledge to know when you can play with just overcards. A bet with two overcards is usually a semi-bluff (you're hoping to win the pot right there, but have chances of improving to the best hand). Most low-limit games are sufficiently loose and passive that a semi-bluff won't work, so betting is not correct.

We believe you are not losing much by folding in this situation if there's a bet ahead of you. If it's checked to you, take a free card and hope you turn top pair.[1] In the situation above, if a queen or king falls on the turn, you probably have the best hand and can bet (or even raise).

Otherwise, don't bother

In the first and second editions of this text, I spilled a bunch of ink describing exceptions to the rule of "don't play overcards." This was a mistake. Many *winning* hold'em players would probably make more money if they routinely threw away overcards that they're playing.

Okay, one exception

If, after all the above, you still need an excuse to play overcards, here it is. Just don't say you weren't warned. You can play two overcards if:

1. You are last to act. Nobody can raise behind you, and

2. You are calling *one* bet, and

3. You have AKs or KQ[2], and

4. You can make top pair or an eight- or nine-out draw on the turn.

Here's an example: you've raised on the button with A♥-K♥ after three calls. The flop comes 9♥-7♣-2♦. The first player bets and one player calls. You can call, hoping to catch an ace, king, or heart on the turn.[3] Note that if you don't get any of these on the turn, you're done.

Now consider the same example, but the first player checks and the second player bets. You may not call — the first player may be waiting to loose a check-raise.

Ace-King

AK ("big slick") is a problem hand for many players. After all, if you don't make top pair on the flop, then you've got two over-

---

[1]This is particularly important on the Internet, where players love to check-raise.

[2]Note that KQ can pick up an open-end straight draw on the turn if there's a jack or ten on the flop. AK can not do this, so it needs to be suited and pick up a flush draw on the turn.

[3]If you think that a raise will get you a free card on the turn, do so.

cards. Note that the rules described above apply to AK if there is a bet in front of you. Suppose you have raised with AK, but don't flop top pair and either you have to act first or it's checked to you. The following set of rules is a good start to your hold'em career:[4]

- If you have one opponent, bet the flop, bet the turn, and check the river (assuming, of course, you don't improve). If you get raised at any point, fold.

- If you have two opponents, bet the flop. If you lose one on the flop, then bet the turn, check the river. If both still remain on the turn, check and fold.

- If you have more than two opponents, check and fold (or take a free card if you're last to act).

This is obviously a simplified approach to poker and will require adjustment and fine-tuning as you progress. But it is a good first path to take through some swampy ground.

A final word of warning

In tighter games, you can use the flop to decide the chances that you're up against two pair already. However, in a no fold'em hold'em game, many players are capable of showing you *any* two cards. For instance, in a tighter hold'em game you'd be more inclined to play overcards with a flop of T-5-2 since it would be unlikely somebody already had two pair. In lower limit games, you will see people win big pots with T5. This is another reason why it's a bad play to continue with just overcards in low-limit hold'em games.

You will routinely see your opponents continue playing (even calling a raise cold) with two overcards to the flop. You will also occasionally be sitting on the sidelines watching when your overcards would have made the best hand. Have faith, and throw them away the next time, too. For low-limit hold'em players, flopping two overcards is a marginal case of our next topic: what to do when the flop misses you completely.

---

[4]I need to thank Barry Tanenbaum for these rules.

Playing When the Flop Misses You

In completing our discussion of how to play on the flop, we need to remind you that this, unfortunately, will be the most frequent result of the flop: you get a very small piece of it, or less.

You'll flop second or bottom pair with no overcards. Three to a flush or straight and nothing else. One overcard.

Your opponents will routinely call a bet in this situation, hoping to pick up a little more on the turn. This is where decisive action can save you a lot of money:

Fold and be done with it.

We have discussed essentially every case in which you can play beyond the flop. Every other time, your pre-flop investment is gone. Forget about it. Watch the rest of the hand. See how your opponents play, figure out what you would do in a similar situation. Get up and stretch, drink a glass of water. However, do not just throw in a loose call on the flop to see what happens next. This discipline alone will take you a long way toward becoming a winning hold'em player.

Bluffing on the flop

Suppose the flop misses you completely, but it looks very ragged and you think it might have missed everybody else too. Is this a good time to bluff? In a bigger limit game, the answer might well be yes. In a low-limit hold'em game, you're probably wasting your money. We will go into more detail about bluffing in a later chapter, but for now, consider what we said above. Many of your opponents don't think twice about calling a bet on the flop — they just throw the chips in. Against that kind of opposition, a bluff is simply not profitable. It makes many more *value* bets profitable (i.e., when you have a good or great hand), but trying to represent a hand you don't have won't work often enough to be worth it.

Free Cards and the Importance of Position

As you advance in your poker career, you will develop an arsenal of subtle plays and tricks to use on your opponents. Unfortunately, you won't be able to practice them much in low-limit hold'em games — they simply won't work. However, there is one very powerful play that works quite well in low-limit games — the *free card*.

The free card play is simply raising in late position with a hand that's not likely to be the best at the moment. Your intent is to freeze up bettors in front of you on the next card, giving you the option of betting, or checking and seeing the following card for free. In the $3-$6 game, you've put in an extra $3 bet so you don't have to call $6 on the turn. Every time this play works for you, *it saves you $3*.

A classic example

You are on the button with

and are the fifth caller. Then the small blind raises and everybody calls. Now the flop comes

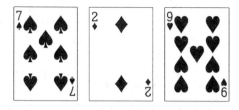

There is a bet and two callers in front of you. With 14 bets in the pot, you have an easy call. If the turn is an eight, you have the nuts. A jack or ten may give you the best hand, and if a diamond falls, you pick up a flush draw. If you raise (instead of calling), the players in front of you may check on the turn. Of course, if you get lucky and turn the straight or top pair, you bet. Otherwise, you check and see the river card for free. This play is almost always successful in passive low-limit games and has enormous value to you.

Other good opportunities to use the free card play:

- Second pair with an overcard kicker and perhaps a backdoor straight or flush draw. Suppose you have A♣-9♣ in late position and the flop comes 9♥-Q♣-2♥. If there is a bet in front of you and you are in last position or (particularly) feel that a raise will knock out any player(s) behind you, seriously consider raising. While it's likely you're up against a queen, it's worth a shot to catch a nine, ace, or backdoor flush draw.[1]

- Flush draw in late position when there's a bet in front and callers in between. You'd rather not call a bet on the turn if you don't make your flush; raise on the flop, hoping to make the original bettor check on the turn. You probably aren't giving up a raise if you make your flush on the turn. Many players will freeze up at the sight of a third suited card and check anyway.

---

[1]Depending on the pot size and other factors, you may need to call a bet on the river with your second pair and ace kicker.

Raising here also has some deceptive value. Your opponents may assume that you had top pair or something when you raised on the flop (which you easily could have). Now when the flush card hits, they may bet at you, representing the flush. Of course, your raise on the turn shows them they're mistaken.

The importance of position

You see that to make the free card play, you must be in late position, preferably last to act. This points out yet another reason why you have to pay such close attention to your position. Many hands that will simply not pay up front will make money for you in late position because you can use the free card play.

An added benefit of the free card raise may be to knock out players between you and the button. If there is one player behind you and you think your raise on the flop will knock him out, that's all the more reason to raise. "Buying the button" is an important tactic in making the hand go the way you want.

Taking the free card

Sometimes you successfully make a free card play, but then are tempted to bet when they all check to you on the turn. Don't do it. Barry Tanenbaum calls this one of the ten most frequent mistakes that limit hold'em players make (page 248), and he's right.

Yes, by checking you're probably giving up the pot if you don't hit your draw on the river. But sometimes you give up pots when you don't make your hand and have nothing; poker is like that.

If you need a free card, and they offer one, take it.

Defending against the free card

Unfortunately, you have to take your turn in the early and middle positions. Sometimes you will bet on the flop and get raised by a player in late position. If you think he's capable of trying to get a free card, what should you do? If you believe you have the best hand, re-raise immediately, or call and then bet on the turn. As you can see, this is an awkward situation since he may have you beaten, and you're just giving him more chances to raise. However, you should be aware of the possibility that somebody is trying to get a free card, and defend against that.

The difficulty of defending against the free card shows both how powerful a play it is and the importance of having good position. Remember that when you're thinking about playing marginal hands in early position before the flop.

Confrontations on the Flop

Warning: you will have to make full use of your experience and judgment in situations such as we describe below. Treat the following as guidelines, not rules.

Ideally, if you're going to play a hand after the flop, you want to take control of it. You should be doing the raising (unless of course you've flopped a monster), and generally making other players do what you want.

Dealing with a maniac

With weak loose players (calling stations), you can usually accomplish this. However, against a maniac, it's often impossible. He will happily re-raise you with a draw, any pair, or just on a bluff. You will find that a maniac is often being controlled by his ego — he wants to put in the last raise, or bluff you out of a pot with nothing. When you get into a situation like this, it's often best to bend and let him take control. Especially if you have position, you can afford to do this. Suppose you have

and raise after four players call. The flop comes

Two players check and the third bets. You raise, the first two players drop. Now the original bettor re-raises, and the player between you drops. The bettor could have a queen with a smaller kicker, two pair, a set, or even just a draw.

If the turn card is not a club and he checks, you should bet for value. Many players will put in a lot of bets with a flush draw on the flop (although you know this is not correct heads-up), so his check on the turn may be a clue to that. If the turn is not a club and he continues to bet, call again.[1] If the turn is a club and he bets, you may have to drop. If he has a flush, you're drawing dead, and will have to call again on the river. Even if he doesn't have the flush, he's willing to bet into a possible flush, and that implies some more strength. If the flush card comes and he checks, you've got a difficult choice. You'd hate to give him a free card if he has a singleton club. But if you bet and he check-raises, then you have to fold if he's a rational player.[2]

The situation is slightly different if you have to act first. Suppose the hand went the same way, but you check-raised on the flop, and the original bettor made it three bets, narrowing the field to just two of you. It's unfortunate that you're out of position, but giving a free card with this draw-rich board is almost unthinkable. You have to bet. If he raises again, then call, and check and call the river. If he just calls, I would bet the river too, unless

---

[1] Actually, a better play here may be to raise the turn, and plan to check the river unless you improve.

[2] If your man is the least bit "unreliable," then you simply can't give up top pair with an ace kicker. If you get check-raised on the turn by somebody like that, you grit your teeth, call, and then call on the river.

something terrifying such as the K♣ comes, in which case you should check and call.

A general navigational tool

Frequently you will be in the following situation: you have a strong, but not overwhelming hand (top pair with the best or second best kicker is a perfect example). You have done what you are supposed to do — bet and raised. But one opponent is pushing back hard, suggesting that he can beat you. Here is a good goal:

Plan to get one bet per round into the pot.

This is relatively easy to do if you have position on your opponent. If he bets, you call; if he checks, you bet. If you're out of position, it's more difficult, but often the more aggressive players will oblige you simply by betting every time you check.[3]

A hand like this one is good enough that you want some money in the pot, but not worth going to war if an opponent is saying (via his betting) that he has you beaten. But it's too good to fold unless there's lots of multi-way action and a scary board.

When you have a great hand

If you have the nuts, and it's not possible that somebody has the same hand but is drawing, put in a lot of bets (at least four or five) before stopping. For instance, if you have

---

[3]Mike Caro teaches an important point about circumstances like this: if you're not sure you're calling a better hand or a bluff, don't make it obvious that you're going to call all the way. In a live game, don't hang your chips out over the table, and online, don't call instantly after he bets. If your opponent is betting a better hand, such antics won't slow him down. But they just might prevent him from bluffing (or value-betting a worse hand), which is where you get *your* value.

and the flop comes

you can put five or six bets. However, if you had A♣-J♣ instead of A♦-J♣, your opponent could have the big straight *and* a diamond draw as well. If so, he's "free rolling" on you. Now you have to stop at about four bets and hope that no diamonds show up.

If you have a great hand but don't have the nuts, then you have to back off earlier. You're not going to fold the hand (even on the turn and river because the pot has gotten huge). However, you need to consider the possibility that you're beaten. Suppose you have

and the flop comes

If you get into a raising war with two or more opponents, don't be afraid to put in the last raise. However, if you are heads-up, and your opponent keeps raising, at some point you have to worry about pocket jacks. After four or five bets, back off and then check and call through the river. If your opponent checks, bet.

Note that many players will play JT or 55 as strongly as you would play JJ, so you may still be winning, but you don't want to put in too many raises without the nuts.

Now, suppose you have the guaranteed nuts. Perhaps you have A♠-T♠ and the flop is J♠-8♠-4♠. You get into a raising war with a single opponent and, for whatever reason, he keeps raising. Once you're *absolutely* sure you have the nuts (don't forget to check for a possible straight flush), how many raises should you put in? The best chance your opponent can have here is that he flopped a set. If so, he'll make a full house or better to beat your flush about a third of the time: you are a 2:1 favorite. Nevertheless, if he *does* get lucky and improve, you lose a lot of money. Thus, your decision here is somewhat personal. If you are willing to invest all your chips in a very positive situation (which this is), go ahead and raise until he stops raising or one of you is out of chips. If not, stop at whatever point you feel comfortable. If you still have the nuts on the turn, you can make the same decision again, knowing you're an almost 4:1 favorite. As we'll discuss later, if you have the nuts on the river, don't stop raising.

Play on the Turn

In general, your play on the turn and river will be more straightforward than that on the flop.

If you have the best hand

If you feel you have the best hand, continue to bet it, especially if you are concerned about draws. For instance, suppose you have

and raised on the flop, which was

Two players (including the original bettor) called your raise. If the next card is not a jack, an overcard, or a club, you should bet again. A player with a jack will probably call, and you cannot give overcards and flush draws a free card.

If a scary card does fall, you have a more awkward situation. You can't be sure if it helped your opponents or not. Giving somebody with A♣-K♦ a free card when a small club falls is a terrible mistake, but you will have to do that sometimes. Try not to be paranoid about the nuts always being up against you; if you think you still have the best hand, go ahead and bet.

If you're not sure you have the best hand

If you are afraid you might not have the best hand, and you aren't too worried about free cards, then it's better to check. For instance, suppose you have

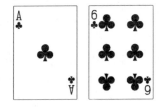

in late position, and the flop comes

It's checked to you, you bet, and two people call. Now the 8♣ comes on the turn and they both check again. You should go ahead and bet again.[1] There are too many cards in the deck that could beat you and you can't afford to give a free card. You're not particularly delighted about the situation (betting top pair with an almost nonexistent kicker). But if your opponents have something like T9 and 43, then there are ten cards in the deck that will beat you on the river; you can't let the field draw that many for free. And the more opponents you have, the more important it is that you bet. If you get check-raised on the turn, fold with a clear conscience.

---

[1]In the first two editions, I said to check here. Barry Tanenbaum showed me the light.

Note that if you end up with one opponent in this situation, it's best to check. This is the "way in front or way behind" situation. One likely scenario is that you have your opponent drawing at two outs (e.g., he has TT) or five outs (e.g., he has T9). The other is that he has a better ace and you have three outs (if that). Since you're not sure if you're giving a free card or taking one, and the river card is unlikely to change the outcome of the hand, it's fine to check here.

Scare cards

A "scare card" is one that is likely to change who is in front. For instance, suppose you have T♠-J♠, and the flop is 7♣-T♣-8♠. There is a bet and you raise. While you don't have a huge hand, this is a fine play. But now the K♣ comes on the turn. That is a canonical scare card. Suddenly you no longer have top pair, and a flush is possible. If you have just one opponent, then you should continue betting (but fold to a raise). If you have more than one opponent, and they are betting and calling (or raising) there is no reason to continue in the hand.

Note that even if your hand "improves," your overall situation may have worsened. Consider the above situation, but the turn card is the J♣. Now you have top two pair, but any nine makes a straight and again the club flush is possible. In some senses this is a more difficult situation for you because you have four outs to a huge full house; you can't fold quite as easily. You are about an 11:1 dog to make your full house on the river. Again, if you have just a single opponent, that player will have to show you a better hand. If you have more than one opponent and they are putting bets in the pot, you should assume that you are beaten somewhere. Then simply decide if you're getting the necessary 11:1 odds (or implied odds) to call a bet.

Drawing hands

Your hands that were marginal calls on the flop have now become clear in one direction or the other. Suppose you are in late position with

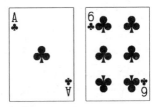

and six people take the flop for one bet. The flop is

There is a bet and two calls and then you call. This is not an obvious call, but it's not a bad play either. However, the turn makes your decision easy: if you get a six or an ace, you raise; if you get a club, you call;[2] otherwise, you fold.

Most of your drawing hands will fall into similar situations by the turn. You can almost surely stay with strong flush and straight draws; it's likely you'll be getting the right odds to draw. However, if the board is paired, you have to be getting much better odds. If the third card of a suit hits on the turn, throw away your straight draw without a second thought.

Betting draws on the turn

There are times when it makes sense to bet a draw on the turn. Particularly if you're down to one or two opponents and you think there's any chance at all they will fold, it might be worth betting. For instance, if you flopped a straight draw and turned a flush draw, or vice versa, you may have as many as 15 outs. If so, you're only about a 2:1 dog to win on the river, so you should bet. After all, you may win the pot on the turn, you may hit one of your outs, or your opponents may get tired of you betting all the time and fold on the river. A small pair with an overcard kicker

---

[2]As mentioned before, in a tighter game, if you picked up a flush draw on the turn, a semi-bluff raise would be a powerful play.

and a flush draw often deserves a bet on the turn if there's any chance that you can win the pot right there.

See if you can bet your draw on the turn for value. If not, ask yourself if there's a chance you might win the pot right there. If neither of those conditions holds, you should usually take a free card if you can get one.

Raising on the turn

You will probably not be doing as much raising on the turn as some of your opponents. They will often slow play strong hands. As we discussed earlier, you are usually better off raising or check-raising on the flop. Once you have shown that strength early in the hand, your opponents will often check to you on the turn.

However, there will be times when you slow play a hand, or improve your hand on the turn. If so, you should almost always start raising on the turn rather than wait for the river to raise. By raising on the turn, you are getting the most possible value for your strong hand, and forcing drawing hands to pay extra while there are cards yet to come. If you wait until the river, people who missed draws are not going to call a single bet, much less a raise.

Another time to raise on the turn is when you're going to call a bet on the river anyway, but could improve to a hand that is worth betting. For instance, suppose you have A♣–9♣ in late position, and get a flop of A♦–6♣–3♣. Now you and two other players cap the pot. In spite of your marginal kicker, you're committed to calling a bet on the river even if you don't improve, because of the size of the pot. Particularly if the pot gets heads-up on the turn, you should raise, hoping to force your opponent into checking the river. Now if you improve (catching a nine or a club), you bet, otherwise you check. This way, you lose the same two big bets if you don't have the best hand, but win a third big bet if you improve. Also, this looks like "gambling" to your opponents, and mars your disciplined image.

If you are raised on the turn

This is a very difficult situation to handle correctly. A very common scenario is that you have top pair or an overpair that you bet on the turn, but you get raised. Your opponent is clearly telling you that he can beat top pair.

There are a few things to consider at this point. If your opponent is a very tight, predictable player, you can be fairly sure that he has you beaten. If so, and you don't have the proper odds to draw, you can fold immediately. If the pot is large, you can call and see if you improve on the river (by making two pair or trips). If not, you can fold (your opponent will almost surely bet on the river).

You also need to think about the card that hit on the turn. Was it apt to have made the raiser two pair, or was he possibly slow playing two pair that he had flopped? If the turn card was the second of a suit, is your opponent creative enough to raise when he picked up a flush draw?

Of course, there are some situations that are much easier to fold. If the turn was the third of a suit or an overcard to your pair, then it's much easier to fold without calling the raise. However, in many situations, you won't be so sure about what your opponent has, and the pot will be fairly large. In some of those cases, you have to grit your teeth and call the raise and the (very probable) bet on the river. If you fold every time you are raised with an unimproved pair on the turn, you're giving up too much.

Calling raises in multi-way pots

In *most* situations, one pair (even a big pocket overpair to the board) is no longer in front if somebody is raising on the turn in a multi-way pot. This is a very difficult situation to handle correctly because the pot has often gotten quite large. But in general, if you have opponents raising and calling raises on the turn (or the river, for that matter), your top pair or overpair is probably not the best hand. Furthermore, you may be drawing extremely thin, or dead. Give serious consideration to giving up even powerful hands such as pocket aces and kings here.

Play on the River

$\mathbf{P}$lay on the river is somewhat cut-and-dried. After all, there are no more draws possible — they got there or they didn't. Nobody is trying to get any free cards. Implied odds are gone.[1] The pot has gotten almost as big as it's ever going to get; the pot odds that people are receiving for their calls are as good as they're going to get.

There are two important distinctions involving play on the river:

1.   Are you heads-up with a single opponent, or is the pot being played multi-way?

2.   Do you have position on your opponent(s)?

If you're heads-up and act first

The most important thing I can say about this:

Bet.

That is, if you've been betting the whole way because you think you have the best hand, put out that one last bet. Let's say you raise with A♣-Q♥, and get a flop of Q♣-7♦-2♥. You bet, your opponent (on the button) raises, and you make it three bets, which he calls. The turn is the 4♥, you bet, and he calls. If the 6♥ comes on the river, *bet*. Sure, maybe he made a backdoor flush. But there's a much better chance that he has something like KQ or QJ, and will certainly call your bet.

---

[1]If you don't understand why implied odds are gone after the river card is dealt, please review the subsection on implied odds, beginning on page 34.

Or suppose you've been trying to hit a hand and get there. Don't get fancy — bet.[2] For instance, suppose you are on the big blind with K♥-T♥, there are two late position callers, and you check. The flop comes 9♦-6♥-2♥, you check, the next player bets, and the third folds. You call. The turn is the 3♠; you check and call his bet. If the river is a king, a ten, or a heart, *you bet*. Every one of those cards should worry him. It's either an overcard to the board or makes a flush. What do you think he's going to do when he's worried? He's going to check. He's not going to bet and then call your very sneaky check-raise. No, he's going to check and make you look silly. When you make your hand and have to act first, bet.

Now, suppose you raise with A♣-Q♥, and get a flop of Q♦-7♦-2♠. You bet, get raised, and re-raise, which the raiser calls. The turn is the T♥, you bet and are called. Now the dreaded 8♦ comes on the river. You have two options: you can bet, and if you get raised, almost always call. Or you can check and call. If your opponent tends to bluff too much, you should check and call (giving him a chance to bluff at you). If you don't think this opponent is capable of raising with a flush draw on the flop, then the diamond shouldn't be too scary and you should bet.

If you are betting a strong one-pair hand and get raised on the river (in a heads-up pot), you should call virtually all the time. In fact, here's a good rule:

If, in a heads-up pot, you bet an overpair or top pair with
an ace or king kicker, and are raised, <u>always</u> call.

If you're going to fold in a situation like this, do it when you are making a "thin" value bet. Perhaps you were betting second pair, or top pair with a very weak kicker. Even in those cases, you should fold only rarely — perhaps 10% of the time.[3]

---

[2]Barry Tanenbaum calls "Not betting your hand when you make it" one of the ten most common errors that limit hold'em players make. See page 248.

[3]The correct game-theoretical frequency is to fold once in N times where N is the number of big bets in the pot. That is, if there are 12 big bets in the pot when you are raised, you should fold 1/12 of the time in situations such as you are in. 10% is a close enough approximation.

You're heads-up and act last

Obviously, this is the easier situation to play, in every respect. The same advice, however, holds. If you've been betting the (presumed) best hand, and your opponent checks on the river, *bet again*. The most common reason people check on the river is that *they don't like their hand very much*.

Players give up far too many bets on the river by checking down strong single pair hands. Don't do it.

Just as I described in the previous subsection, if you are check-raised, call with all of your very strong one-pair hands (and better) and fold 10% of the time with weaker hands that you were value betting. Always fold if you were bluffing.

Now, suppose your opponent bets (instead of checking, like he's supposed to). Well, if you missed a draw, you fold. If you hit a draw, you raise. If you had a hand that was "pretty good" (e.g., one pair), then you call. Of course, if you had a pretty good one-pair hand and had position on your opponent, then you should be wondering why you let him take control of the hand and keep betting.

One possible reason for this is that you have a hand such as top pair with a medium kicker. If you raised on the flop and got three-bet, then go ahead and call on the turn and river.

Sometimes you have to call with marginal hands simply because the pot has gotten large. For instance, suppose you have A♠-9♠ and got a flop of Q♠-6♦-2♠. It is checked to you on the flop, you bet, but get a single caller. The turn misses your flush (2♣) and you both check. Now the 9♥ comes on river. If your opponent bets, you should call. Your check on the turn indicated weakness, but you "accidentally" made second pair on the river.

Note that if you don't hit that pair, you shouldn't call a bet. Sure, your opponent may be bluffing, but even some bluffs (e.g., AK) beat your hand. If you are absolutely "sure" that your opponent is bluffing, then you have to raise and hope he folds. This is a high variance play and you should use it most sparingly (not more than 5% of the time).

But in general, if you have any kind of reasonable hand (top pair or even second pair) and a single opponent bets into you, you should call 90% of the time.

Multi-way pot, and you act first

Obviously, the more opponents you have, the stronger hand you need to bet. However, if you can reasonably assign hands to your opponents and still like your chances, then bet. For instance, suppose you raise with A♦-K♣, and get a A♠-6♥-4♠ flop. You bet, get a caller, and then the button raises. You three-bet and both players call. The turn is the 4♥, you bet, and they both call. The river is another innocuous card — the 9♦. Well, it's fair to assign one of them a worse ace and the other a flush draw. Then you bet and expect to get one caller.

If you have more than two opponents, then things become muddier. Since you have a strong hand and would like to see a showdown, check and see what develops. If it comes back two bets cold to you, then you have an easy fold. If you can call one bet and close the betting, then do so.

If you bet, the first opponent raises, and the second opponent calls two bets cold, you can fold a single pair without hesitation. You will occasionally lay down the best hand that way, but you will make money by folding every time.

Multi-way pot, and you act in the middle

If it's checked to you, you can mostly ignore the first player and pretend you act first against the opponent(s) behind you. Again, bet your strong hands (including good one-pairs) against one or two opponents behind you if you can put them on hands you beat.

If there are more than two players behind you, don't bet a hand smaller than two pair.

You must have a stronger hand to call a bet if you're in the middle of multi-way action on the river. That's because the player(s) behind you can raise or overcall.[4] A weak top pair or strong sec-

---

[4]An "overcall" is a call after one or more players has already called.

ond pair should be folded here even though you'd call with it heads-up.

You can *occasionally* make a positional raise to force out a player behind you. For instance, suppose you have top pair with a mediocre kicker. The first player to act bets, but you suspect he's bluffing. If you think you can force out a better one pair behind you with a raise, then go for it. Don't call though — either raise or fold.

Conversely, if you have a strong hand, but not a monster, you may prefer trying to collect one bet from two players rather than two bets from one. Suppose you made a straight, but the flush got there at the same time. The first player bets out, and you're in the middle. If you raise, you're may run into a re-raise from either player (which will make you unhappy). But by calling, you might get an overcall from the player behind you. If your hand is good, you win two bets, but if not, you lose only one.

Multi-way pot, and you act last

If it's checked all the way to you, then bet your strongest hands as you would heads-up. Don't bet the hands that would be borderline bets heads-up (e.g., top pair with a nine kicker). Your opponents will be nervous with multi-way action and will check slightly stronger hands than they would normally.

If there's a bet and it's folded to you, then call as you would in a heads-up situation. But you must have a substantially stronger hand to overcall, just as you would if you were in the middle and had players yet to act behind you.

Note that if there is a check and then a bet in front of you, you're acting somewhat in the middle. The check implies weakness, but that player could still check-raise. So you must have a slightly stronger hand to call than you would if you knew your call closed the betting.

Again, don't call with one-pair hands if two or more players are willing to put in two or more bets. If the first player bets and the second player raises, then fold any one-pair hand.

Multi-way pots and marginal hands

In case I didn't make it clear enough in the previous paragraphs:

Fold marginal hands in multi-way pots on the river.

Betting a hand you'll have to call

Sometimes, pot odds will demand that you call a bet on the river, even though you don't think you have the best hand. In situations such as that, you may want to bet in case you can get a crying call. For instance, suppose you are on the big blind with A5s. There is an early position raise, three people cold call the two bets, and you call for one more bet. The flop is A-8-3 with none of your suit, and you check. This is a good play because you'd like to see how your four opponents are going to behave. But the pre-flop raiser checks too, as does everybody else.

Now the turn is an offsuit jack, and you bet. Again, this is a fine play — your top pair with no kicker may actually be best. The pre-flop raiser folds, two of the other opponents fold, but the fourth opponent calls.

The river is a six. You have a pair of aces, but literally no kicker (your best hand is a pair of aces, then jack-eight-six). If you check and that opponent bets, you have to call; there is simply too much money in the pot to fold top pair. But if you check, somebody with a jack (for example) will almost certainly check the hand down. By checking, you are in danger of paying off better hands and not collecting from worse ones.

So go ahead and bet. If you get raised, fold ten percent of the time (as I discussed above).

Note that if your bet on the turn produced three callers, then checking the river is the best play. You just don't have enough ammunition to shoot at that many enemies.

Raising forever with the best hand

Once in a while, you will get into a raising war on the river with a single opponent. You have the nuts, and yet he keeps raising. Once you're *sure* you have the nuts, how many raises should you put in? If you cannot be tied, then of course you should continue raising until your opponent stops or one of you is out of chips. If you could be tied, then you can stop at eight or nine bets. A good dealer will recognize the situation and keep your bets and those of your opponents separate, simplifying the subsequent pot split.[5] If you suspect at *all* that your opponent is overplaying his hand, or doesn't recognize the true nuts, then happily raise until one of you is out of chips. Some players at your table may get upset about this if you do split the pot; ignore them. Even a slim chance that your opponent is wrong justifies unlimited raising.

If the nuts is on the board (e.g., J♥-K♦-T♦-A♠-Q♣), you might occasionally try a bet or raise to knock out oblivious opponents (the pot is split among all remaining players). However, don't take this play too far; very few players will fall for it.

Betting only when you want to be called

Just because you think you have the best hand on the river doesn't mean you should bet. You should only bet on the end if you'll have the best hand most of the time *when you're called*. For instance, suppose you have

and when the 3♠ falls on the river, the board looks like

---

[5]Of course, when you're playing online, pot splits happen instantly, but all on-line sites I'm aware of have a limit of three raises, even heads-up.

You had bet on the flop and turn because you feared that your opponent was on a diamond flush draw (or perhaps a gutshot draw with a singleton king or queen). Now if you bet, one of two things will happen. If your opponent missed his draw he will throw his hand away. Otherwise, there is a very good chance that he has you beaten (perhaps with an ace and higher kicker) and is checking and calling. In this situation, you will only be called if you are beaten, so you simply check your hand down.

Note that we are *not* talking about bluffing here. A bluff is a bet when you are fairly sure you don't have the best hand. In this case, you think you may well have the best hand, but you cannot bet it. Of course, if you think you can make some better hands fold, it may be to your advantage to bet. However, in low-limit hold'em games, this is rarely the case. If you think there's a fair chance that you have the best hand, then few of your opponents will be willing to fold a *better* hand.

In cases such as the above, you should be prepared to call a bet if you have to act first and check. Many of your opponents would continue betting your hand in this situation, and they assume you will too. Often when you check and call here, you will have the best hand.

A similar argument applies to raising on the river. If you are pretty sure you have the best hand, then of course you would raise. However, you must ask yourself if an opponent will call your raise with a hand worse than yours. If not, then you should not raise. Also, you have to consider the chance that you'll be reraised. This further reduces the number of hands with which you should raise on the river.

This concept is extremely powerful and many poker players do not understand it. If you can spot these situations and play them correctly, you will save a lot of money over the course of your poker career.

The most important point about playing the river

If you have top pair with a good kicker, an overpair, or better than one pair, and the pot is heads-up, bet.

Quiz on Post-Flop Play

1. Give three reasons why the flop is the most crucial point in a hold'em hand.

2. What is the most common mistake made by low-limit hold'em players on the flop?

3. What is the most important use of the check-raise in low-limit hold'em games?

4. How should you normally play A♠-Q♠ if the flop comes Q♦-J♥-2♣ and you were the only one who raised before the flop?

5. How should you normally play A♠-5♠ in late position if the flop comes A♥-8♦-4♣, there has been no raise before the flop, and you have six opponents?

6. How should you normally play Q♥-Q♣ in early position against five opponents if the flop comes A♣-T♦-4♦ and you put in the only pre-flop raise?

7. If you have T♦-9♦ and the flop comes T♣-9♠-4♣, what should you do, and why?

8. Suppose you have K♥-K♦, you raised before the flop, and six players take the flop, which comes K♣-7♦-2♥. What should you normally do?

9. You have A♣-T♣ on the button. Six people take the flop, which comes J♣-9♦-4♣. There's a bet and three calls in front of you. What should you normally do?

10. You have 9♥-8♥ in late position. There is no raise pre-flop, and five people take the flop, which comes T♦-6♣-3♣. It is checked until the player to your right bets. What should you normally do? Now assume the same situation, but there was one raise pre-flop. What should you normally do?

11. Suppose you have T♣-T♦ in middle position, there is a raise before the flop and five callers. The flop comes T♥-8♥-8♠. How should you normally play? What would be a reasonable alternative play?

12. Suppose you have 5♠-3♦ on the big blind and get to see the flop for "free." The flop comes 4♣-7♣-6♥. You have four opponents. How should you normally play?

13. You have J♦-T♦ on the button and are the fourth caller (no raise). The flop comes 7♣-6♥-2♥. There is a bet and one call in front of you. How should you normally play? Now suppose the flop comes 9♣-4♥-2♦. How does this change the situation?

14. You have 6♠-5♠ in middle position with four opponents, and no raise pre-flop. The flop comes T♣-6♥-3♣. There's a bet and a caller in front of you. What is typically the best play in this situation?

15. You have A♦-A♠ in late position and raise before the flop, ending up with two opponents. The flop comes K♣-T♣-4♦. The first player to act bets, the second folds. You raise and the first player makes it three bets. What would be reasonable plays in this situation?

16. You have Q♣-J♠ on the big blind, and there are five callers including you. The flop comes 8♥-J♦-2♥. You check, as does everybody else until the last player to act, who bets. You check-raise, and the original bettor is the only one to call. Now the T♣ comes on the turn. What should you normally do?

17. You have A♥-9♥ on the button and are one of six callers. The flop comes A♣-3♦-8♣. You bet and get two callers. The turn is the 6♠ — they check, you bet, and they call.

The river card is the J♣ and again they both check. What's probably your best play here?

18. You have A♥-K♦, you raise under the gun, and get three callers. The flop comes 7♥-K♣-3♠. You check, planning to check-raise, but it's checked around. The turn is the J♥, you bet and get one caller. The river is the 8♠. Should you bet or check, and why?

Answers to Quiz on
Post-Flop Play

1. a) The flop determines the likely winner of the hand.

    b) It is when you must make a crucial play/no-play deci-
        sion.

    c) You can gain information using cheaper bets that will al-
        low you to make the correct decisions on later, more ex-
        pensive, cards.

2. Calling bets and raises with hands that have little or no
    chance of winning the pot.

3. To force players to call two bets instead of one, often making
    it incorrect for them to call at all.

4. Aggressively. Bet or raise. Don't hesitate to re-raise the flop
    given the chance. Treat your hand as the best until given al-
    most visual proof that it's not.

5. You have to play very cautiously. Against this many players,
    there's an excellent chance that somebody else has an ace
    with a better kicker. If there is a raise, you should get out. If
    there is a bet and a couple of calls, you should probably get
    out. If it's checked to you, go ahead and bet, hoping to win
    the pot right there.

6. Unfortunately, you can be almost sure that you're beaten. In
    spite of the large pot size, you should check, and fold if
    there's a bet. As you get to later position, if it's checked to
    you, it might be worth an exploratory bet. If you get called
    by more than one or two players, then you should be hesitant
    to put any more money in the pot.

7. You should play very fast. Do whatever is necessary to get lots of bets in on the flop. While you almost assuredly have the best hand, you want to put pressure on the thin draws, such as K♣-Q♥. A monster draw such as Q♣-J♣ is about even money with you. But unless somebody has a set, you are a "money favorite," meaning that you show a profit for every dollar that goes in on the flop. Don't be afraid to get into a raising war, especially with two or more opponents.

8. You should bet or raise immediately on the flop. The flop is just about perfect for you — it's virtually impossible you won't have the best hand on the turn. However, there is so much money in the pot, there's no reason to slow play. Furthermore, after you raised pre-flop, your opponents will expect you to bet, so you haven't given out any information.

9. You should raise. You are about a 2:1 dog to make your flush, so you are actually raising for value here. Also, your raise may get you a free card on the turn, should you need one. Note also that an eight or queen on the turn gives you an open-end straight draw as well; you may be able to bet your draw for value on the turn.

10. In the first case, you can't call with your gutshot straight draw — there are not enough bets in the pot, and you must worry about a raise behind you or a check-raise in front. If there was a raise before the flop, it is a marginal call because the pot has gotten so large. However, realize that you are only drawing at three "clean" outs. The 7♣ may make somebody a club flush, and you still run the danger of a raise or check-raise. To really feel comfortable about this call, you'd want (1) no flush draw, (2) that there was a raise before the flop, and (3) that your call would close the betting.

11. You have flopped a monster hand, and the chance of your being beaten is tiny. However, the pot is huge (10 small bets on the flop), so there's no point in slow playing. On the other hand, slow playing this hand is a reasonable approach — you're not worried about getting beaten, and you're willing to let some lesser hands catch up.

12. In spite of a relatively small pot, you must do everything you can to eliminate opponents immediately. You could be up against a club flush draw or a big straight draw (such as 9♥-8♥). It's even possible you're dead against 85, but that's unlikely. You must bet and/or raise on the flop.

13. Even though you have two overcards, you should fold. You have no backdoor flush chances, and the 7-6 combination on the flop makes two pair more likely. In the second situation, you have backdoor straight and flush chances and there's perhaps less chance that you're already up against two pair. You can call a bet here.

14. You've missed the flop — your second pair with no kicker is useless. Fold immediately.

15. You could call and then call your opponent's bets on the turn and river (assuming he bets). It's possible he has already made two pair or a set, but with this flop you can't fold yet. On the other hand, if you suspect your opponent is raising with a king or a draw, you could raise once more and try to regain control of the hand, forcing him to check on the turn. An alternative is to call and then raise on the turn.

16. You should bet out. You may run into two pair or even a straight, but you have to take that chance on the turn. You don't dare give a heart flush draw a free card, or a jack with a smaller kicker a free card with which to beat you. If the river is an overcard, makes a four-straight, or a flush possible, you should check and call. Otherwise bet.

17. You should typically check. As in the above situation, the board is fairly scary, and you just have one pair with a mediocre kicker. If you bet and get called, you can't be very happy. If an opponent bets into you on the end, you should call. If the river card were the J♦ instead of the flush-completing club, you should bet.

18. Go ahead and bet here. There are many worse hands that will call you. The flop that got checked around may confuse some people; you will probably get called by a worse king and maybe even a jack. Even if you had successfully check-raised the flop, you should continue betting the turn and river.

Section III

Tournaments, the Internet and the "Sit & Go"

Tournaments

Unlike regular "ring" or "live" games, poker tournaments are played with chips that have no cash value. You pay a certain amount of money, known as the "buy-in," and receive tournament chips in exchange. The number of tournament chips you receive doesn't necessarily have any correlation to the amount of money you paid — just think of them as points.[1]

A tournament starts with blinds of a certain level, and then increases those blinds at regular intervals, often doubling them for the first few rounds. As the blind levels increase, players with smaller stacks are quickly forced all-in, and one by one, people bust out. In some tournaments, a player may buy-in again ("rebuy") during the first few blind levels.[2] Otherwise, he is out of the tournament.

In most tournaments, there is a percentage payout. That is, the tournament continues until one person has won all the chips, but the last few people each get a percentage of the total prize pool.

For instance, 100 people might each put up $60 to participate in a limit hold'em tournament. Of that $60, $10 goes to the cardroom or casino that is hosting the tournament, and $50 goes into

---

[1] You will note that throughout the text, I refer to tournament chips as "chips" and not "dollars." They are not dollars; you can't cash them in or spend them. The poker media have purposely blurred the line between these two, presumably because it makes for more excitement. As Mike Caro points out, the ultimate winner of a percentage payback tournament takes a terrible beat: he wins *all* the chips, but receives less than half of the prize pool.

[2] I hold with the school that says that the tournament starts when the rebuys end.

the prize pool, so there's $5000 in the prize pool. Each player receives 500 in tournament chips, and the blinds start at 5 and 10, so the game plays like a regular 10-20 hold'em game. After 30 minutes, the blinds double — now they're 10 and 20, and the game is a 20-40 structure. This continues with the more fortunate players building big stacks and the less fortunate ones busting out. Let's say that our sample tournament has rebuys during the first three blind levels, and 48 players took 57 $50 rebuys (note that some players rebought multiple times). The additional $2850 (57 x $50) is added to the prize pool for a total of $7850.

Before the tournament begins, the hosting club announces the prize structure. For our example, a typical structure might be 40% to the winner, 20% to 2nd place, 10% to third place, 5% to places 4-7, and 3.3% to places 8-10. So the person who busts out when there are six people left in the tournament wins 5% of the total prize pool, or about $390 — not a bad return on a $50 investment (plus any rebuys that player made).[3]

It's the potential of a big win (with a limited downside) that make tournaments wildly popular. Of course, many of those people will sit down in regular games when they bust out of the tournament, and that makes the cardroom happy.

Tournaments have become such a big thing that some people play tournaments exclusively and don't play in ring games. There are even tournament professionals who follow the tournament trail around the country, hoping to make a single big win that will keep them in buy-ins (and groceries) for the next 6-12 months.

Cheap tournaments as practice

Many players like the cheap buy-in tournaments ($25 or less) because it allows them to play a lot of poker and get a lot of experience for a limited amount of money. And, of course, they might just hit a run of cards and make a profit.

I think this is an excellent approach if you have a limited bankroll and have gotten everything you can out of Turbo Texas Hold'em and free online poker.

---

[3]Not as good a return as the ultimate winner makes; he collects $3140, less taxes.

Poker, Computers, and the Internet

In the second edition of this text, I had a brief chapter about poker on computers and the Internet. I put a disclaimer in there because I feared it was unwise to write about computers and the Internet in a book expected to have a shelf life of more than a year or two.

I underestimated the situation. The computer, and more specifically the Internet, has probably changed poker more in the last handful of years than the game had changed since the Civil War.

So here we go again — I'm writing something that is guaranteed to be obsolete within a relatively short period of time. But it's absolutely necessary to discuss the subject because of its huge effect on poker, and more specifically, hold'em.

Learning hold'em on a computer

There is an old saying that you have pay for your poker lessons, but you can pay for them at the table or away from it. Fortunately, you can find lots of computer software to help you learn hold'em (and thus get your lessons at a discount). The dean of all the programs is still "Turbo Texas Hold'em" by Wilson Software. There are versions for both cash games and tournaments, and they allow you to play hold'em against programmable opponents who never tire of your company. You can get statistics about your play, how much you won (or lost), and even hints from an advisor. But no program will make you a professional quality hold'em player. And it's very dangerous to believe that your results against the cyber-players on any program can be extrapolated to how you'll do in a cardroom or in an online game for money. But by playing and learning with Turbo or its kin, you can remove the truly egregious mistakes from your game before they cost you real money.

Playing hold'em on the Internet

When I wrote the first edition of this book in 1994, playing hold'em (or any kind of poker) on the Internet for real money was unimaginable. It is now commonplace.

Playing online poker is amazingly simple. For instance, suppose you want to play at the PokerStars online poker site.[1] You go on the Web to www.pokerstars.com. From there you download a program called the "client." This is a program that you run on your home computer, just as you would a word processor or email program. Once you have downloaded and installed the client, you will have a PokerStars icon on your desktop.

When you double click the icon and start the program, you will be connected to PokerStars over the Internet, and presented with a "Lobby." That lobby is quite analogous to the lobby of a real casino or cardroom. You can choose from hundreds of cash games and tournaments, with stakes and buy-ins ranging from tiny (less than a dollar) to huge ($100-200 hold'em).

As an example, let's say that you want to play $2-4 hold'em. You find the hold'em section of the lobby and then sort the games by stakes to simplify your search. Then you scroll down to the $2-4 games. You will see a list of tables where $2-4 hold'em is being played, the number of players at each table, the length of waiting list (if any), the average number of players seeing each flop, the average pot size, and the number of hands being dealt each hour. These last three numbers give you a quantitative sense of the game's looseness and speed.

---

[1]A reminder of my disclaimer. At this writing, I am the poker room manager at PokerStars. But be assured that while I use PokerStars for the examples, the general ideas and information are applicable to virtually any online poker site.

You can either choose to get on the waiting list for a full game, or select a game that has open seats. If you pick one that has open seats, you will be taken to that table, and may grab any unoccupied seat. You will be asked how much of your account balance you would like to put on the table in chips.[2] Once you are seated and have chips at the table, you'll be offered the chance to post a blind or wait for the big blind, just as you would in a cardroom.

After you post and are dealt in, everything will proceed as it normally would in a regular cardroom. When it is your turn to act, you simply click your mouse on the desired action (check, bet, fold, etc.). At the end of the hand, you will see the pot pushed to the winner, the button moves, and the next hand is (instantaneously) dealt.

Speed of play

The first thing that you'll notice when playing hold'em on the Internet is how much faster it plays than in a live casino setting. This may seem a bit overwhelming right now, since for new players, it looks unimaginably fast even in a "brick and mortar" casino. But let me give you some specific numbers. A fairly competent dealer in Las Vegas or the Los Angeles area can probably get out 30-35 hands an hour. With the new automatic shuffling machines that some casinos are installing, you can shade that toward 40 hands per hour. In comparison, a typical hold'em table online plays 70-80 hands per hour. Also, note that the limiting factor in the speed of a live game is generally the mechanical portions — shuffling, dealing, rake collection, new decks, etc. So a six-person game doesn't go a great deal faster than a nine-person game. However, online, all of this happens in essentially zero time.[3] So as the game gets shorthanded, it speeds up almost linearly with the reduction in players. Don't be surprised to see a six-person game online deal 100 or more hands per hour.

---

[2] I will discuss later how you to get money into your account.

[3] Including players getting "new decks" — a serious time-waster in live games.

Loose games

Wherever I talk about loose games, online hold'em games are likely to be the perfect example. I believe there are three main reasons why online games are looser than their "live" action cousins:

1. You don't have to pick up those precious chips and put them out in the middle of the table. You just click a mouse and you're still in the hand! That physical barrier in the brick and mortar environment seems to prevent at least some loose calls.

2. The creation of micro-limit games (e.g., $.05-$.10) has made it possible for people to play at the same stakes as they do on their kitchen tables — an environment not known for its tight play.

3. Poker on the Internet is new enough that many players are brand new to the game, haven't read the books, and really don't know what they're doing. It's rather like California was when hold'em was first legalized there in 1987 — a whole new population has suddenly been exposed to the game. And they all want to see the next card.[4]

Note that if people can call with the click of a mouse, then raising is just clicking a different button. The anonymity and ease of the Internet can make a normally meek player a raising machine. So aggressive (sometimes maniacal) games are even more prevalent online than they are in the live games.

Notes

At virtually all online poker sites, you can make notes for yourself about your opponents. This is an incredibly valuable feature and you should use it liberally. Be wary of making too strong a judgment about a player based on a single action, but if you catch him looking at 80% of the flops over a two hour period, it's safe to make a note that he's a calling station.[5]

---

[4] Bless their generous hearts.

[5] There are even better ways to track this, and they're coming up later.

Generally those notes will be stored as a file on your home computer (rather than at the poker site), which has both advantages and disadvantages. It means, for example, that you can share those notes with friends if you wish. On the other hand, if you use multiple computers to play on the site, then you'll have to maintain a separate set of notes on each computer (or copy them back and forth to keep them updated).

Playing multiple games

One of the quantum changes in the whole game of poker took place when online sites began offering players the ability to play multiple games at once. A completely impossible feat in a live cardroom,[6] playing two (or more) games at once online is relatively straightforward. It requires focus and concentration, but many players (particularly the professionals) are able to double or triple their hourly earnings simply by bringing up more tables on their screens. Internet poker forums are filled with discussions of dual monitors and other techniques for playing even half a dozen games at once.[7]

Chat and etiquette

All online poker sites provide a feature where you can chat with other players at your table (and often chat at other tables as an observer). Poker is inherently a social game, so the chat is an integral part of the experience. Players have adapted a number of shorthand comments such as "nh" ("nice hand") and "ty" ("thank you"). Like live cardrooms, you'll see some games being played in relative silence, while others seem to be a coffee klatch with a side dish of poker.

While most chat is friendly and enjoyable, there are always a few people who simply don't know how to behave. With the anonymity of the Internet to protect them, they make ugly, disparaging remarks and insults. Or simply use language that no decent person would use in public. Some poker sites take a *laissez-faire* at-

---

[6]Which is not to say it's never been attempted.

[7]The lingo of online poker now contains grammatical catastrophes such as "I'm four-tabling the $5-10 hold'em."

titude toward such behavior; others police it more strictly. The sad fact is that even constant policing (and de-chatting of regular or egregious offenders) doesn't completely eliminate the problem. The "good" news is that virtually all sites give you the ability to turn off chat, either completely, or by specific players.

While I am a poker author and not Judith Martin,[8] I feel obliged to make this comment: if you wouldn't say something to the face of a fellow poker player in live game, why in the world would it be acceptable to say it over the Internet? I could make arguments about happy enjoyable games being more profitable for the good players, and such arguments are valid. But I'll simply say that the world would be a little better off if we all acted like ladies and gentlemen at the poker table, whether the table is wood and metal or simply pixels on a computer screen.

Tracking software

Essentially all online poker sites maintain a database of all the hands that they have dealt (or at least the more recent ones). They make this information available in a format known as a "hand history." It shows every action by each player throughout a hand, the board cards, the eventual winner, etc. You, as a player at the site, can request your hand histories. Obviously this can be an extremely valuable tool to review your results, send your bad beat stories in emails to friends, etc.

However, a new class of software has made hand histories even more valuable. These are "tracking" programs, into which you load those hand histories.[9] They will tell you how much profit you're making from AQo on the button. Whether it's profitable (based on your statistics) to play 44 under the gun.

But just as importantly, these programs tell you how often your opponents see the flop. How often they check-raise. And most importantly, the tracking programs tell you if those opponents

---

[8]Better known by her *nom de plum*, "Miss Manners."

[9]At this writing, the two most popular such programs are "PokerTracker" and "PokerOffice."

are winning or losing players (again, based on your hand history information about them).

It's difficult to overestimate the value of these programs for on-line play.[10] The player who uses one has a huge edge over his opponents who don't. That edge is perhaps as large as the advantage gained by players who read good poker books over those who don't. Imagine this: each time you sit down at a cyber-table to play, you type into a program the screen names of your opponents at the table. Up pops a matrix showing the percentage of time each sees the flop, turn, and river. How much hourly prof-it or loss each makes. Now, imagine your opponent is learning that about you, but you don't know it about him.

In fact, these programs have created a market in hand history da-tabases. Players are buying, selling, and trading these databases so they have more information about more opponents. At this writing, a relatively small percentage of players are using this software, but those who do will show better results than those who don't; it's almost unavoidable.

Bots

Given that you can study hand histories and learn about your op-ponents' play, it's then (in theory) not too great a step to writing a program that actually plays the hands for you. Such a program is referred to as a "bot" (short for "robot").

The tracking programs I described above are simply the first step on the path to creating a bot. You could expand a tracking pro-gram to give you hints about hands your opponent is likely to have. Or that, based on your statistics of his play, he has proba-bility X of having you beaten. From there, you could advance to have the program suggesting courses of action.

Of course, the bot developer's ultimate goal is a complete autom-aton — a program that analyzes the opponents, makes the play-ing decisions, and even moves the mouse and clicks it.

---

[10]One can argue that they're headed down a slippery ethical slope that I'll dis-cuss in the next subsection.

Such programs have been developed, but most are unable to beat the game. Unlike (for instance) chess, poker is a game of incomplete information. A chess player knows his opponent's exact position, and yet the astronomical number of possible move sequences makes the game interesting. In fact, computer programmers have been working on chess bots for decades, and yet have only recently begun to challenge the best chess players.

Note, though, that a computer can play a perfect game of blackjack, even though there's incomplete information. This is because the dealer's strategy is fixed — the dealer can't arbitrarily decide if he's going to hit or stand at some point. It is merely a question of computing the odds based on the cards in the deck and selecting the best play given those odds.

Poker is a game of incomplete information *and* variable strategy. Your opponent has one or more cards unknown to you, and can vary his play. This makes it much more difficult to teach a computer to play the game. And the good news (unless you're writing a hold'em bot) is that limit hold'em is one of the most complex forms of poker.

Also, poker sites have ways of detecting bots. I'm not going to discuss those techniques here (I'm not interested in helping bot developers avoid detection), but they do exist and are improving.

In summary, there may be a handful of profitable bots playing online, but they are less of a threat to your bankroll than the expert human player.

As an afterthought: is using a bot cheating? My personal belief is that it's not. The bot is using only information that's available to other players; it's simply using more of it, more efficiently. That said, bots are not good for online poker, and I believe that poker sites have a right (and indeed, an obligation) to remove any bots they find. It is much like the wars between casinos and blackjack card counters. Each is a legitimate moneymaking enterprise that must spend some of its energy outsmarting the other.

Cheating

When online poker got started, many people (myself included) worried that cheating would be so rampant that the games couldn't possibly be beatable. After all, two (or more) players could sit on the phone, an instant message service, or even in the same room, sharing hole card information, and in general figuring out the best way to cheat other players.

Fortunately, this dire outcome hasn't happened. Of course, there is some cheating of this sort — it's unavoidable. But the online sites have found ways to short-circuit the cheaters. As a trivial example, sites can prohibit players using the same IP address[11] from sitting at the same table. They can use special software applications to review hand histories and look for signs of collusion (two players working together as a team). And there are many other collusion-catching techniques that had best stay in the hands of the poker sites, not the colluders.

From my perspective as poker room manager at PokerStars.com, I daily watch the battle between the good and bad guys. While I have no illusions that the cheaters and would-be cheaters are ever going to give up, I am encouraged by the general climate. The level of cheating (compared to the number of players simply doing their best to win fairly) is extremely low. Thousands of honest players are making very good profits, and some are making a very good living playing poker online.

My advice to you about avoiding online cheating is this: be observant, but not paranoid. Realize that the vast majority of players are honest, and that if you outplay them, you'll get the money. If you see something that really doesn't look right, contact the site where you're playing. One of the great beauties of hand histories is that they provide permanent evidence of any wrong-doing, and a good poker site will not hesitate to review hand histories if a player expresses concern.

---

[11]Practically speaking, this means that the two computers are in close physical proximity.

Site financial integrity

From the beginning of their existence, online poker sites have battled some perceptions that they're not honest enterprises. Unfortunately, there have been a couple of isolated instances in which sites closed down and took their players' money.

The good news is that as I write this (fall of 2004), the industry has matured significantly. The sites that have survived the initial shake-up are much more secure. They are professionally managed businesses that are in for the long haul. The site that I work for, PokerStars, keeps its player accounts completely separated from corporate operating capital, and I assume others do as well.[12] I believe that deposits in the well-funded mature poker sites are quite safe.

Shuffling and hacking

Poker players are a notoriously suspicious lot, and any time they take a particularly bad beat or experience a long losing streak, they begin wondering if there's a conspiracy against them.[13] This tendency has been exacerbated by the anonymous nature of online poker. You can't see a dealer — in fact, there is no human dealer, just cards popping up on a computer monitor.

Poker-related online discussion groups and coffee-shop gatherings are filled with claims of ineffective shuffles, hacked sites, and overt deck-rigging by the sites themselves.

There are two fundamental categories of these concerns: the site is incompetent (either at shuffling and dealing the virtual deck or at securing their games), or the site is purposely cheating players.

I believe these claims (both categories) are completely groundless. I'll discuss the first category here and the other in the next subsection.

---

[12]Violating this basic principle of fiduciary responsibility is what got one of the early online sites in trouble.

[13]They rarely look inward and review their own play. This is, of course, the first place one should look.

First, let's consider the idea that the sites don't shuffle the deck correctly or are being hacked by outsiders. There is a precedent for this concern. In 1999, the largest existing online poker site had an exploitable random number generation (RNG) algorithm.[14] They made the mistake of publishing the algorithm just to prove how secure it was. But a team of computer experts inspected it and determined that it was not secure. They developed a program that could display the cards that were in other players' hands and those that were going to appear on the board. Fortunately, they alerted the site (and published a paper) rather than exploiting the flaw for their financial gain.

But that was five years ago and, needless to say, the online poker sites have learned their lesson from that incident. They now use cryptographically secure RNGs to shuffle the deck. And some sites use actual random events (such as thermal noise and user mouse movement) to add to the randomness of their shuffle. Producing a thoroughly random (and evenly distributed) shuffle is a mathematically solved problem, the techniques are well known, and the online poker sites have adopted these techniques. It should be obvious that these shuffles are dramatically better than you'll ever get in a live casino.

Note also that time is massively compressed in online poker. Consider a poker veteran who has played in the L.A. area cardrooms since they legalized hold'em in 1987. That's 17 years of getting 30-35 hands per hour. He knows how often he should see "set over set" on the flop (not very), straight flushes (more rare), and mind-bending events, such as pocket threes beating KK after a flop of K44 (almost never — it's a 989:1 shot). Now he begins playing online. In fact, veteran that he is, he's capable of playing three limit hold'em games at once. He's now seeing 200-300 hands per hour — 7-10 times more hands than he saw before. Most of us are not psychologically prepared for that shift. Now the "bizarre" events are happening an order of magnitude more frequently. Rather than one straight flush per year, he gets one a

---

[14]An RNG is the fundamental building block to any computer algorithm to shuffle a virtual deck of cards.

month. All of the moderately large poker sites are likely dealing at least one of those brutal 989:1 runner-runner beats daily.[15] This shift in the sheer volume of hands being dealt fuels the claims of bad shuffling, since people are now routinely seeing things that used to cause the entire cardroom to stand up and take notice.

The other concern that players express is that somehow other players can see their cards (or predict future board cards). Again, this is almost impossible. All the online sites encrypt the card values as they're sent from the site's server to the client on the player's computer. So simply catching the data packets on the Internet wouldn't do it. Hacking into the site itself would be much harder, bordering on the impossible. They have layers and layers of security around the game dealing servers. The probability of somebody successfully hacking into an online poker site and determining other players' cards (or future board cards) is essentially zero. Worry much more about being hit by lightning.[16]

Site honesty

The other half of the conspiracy theories are about the sites themselves purposely cheating players. The claims range from the unlikely to the completely bizarre. I won't try to cover all the possible theories, but will give a general overview, and then my thoughts on the subject.

The "action flop" theory holds that a site looks (via a program) at what cards players are holding and then produces a flop that multiple players will like. This drives up the action, and thus the rake. The "cash-out curse" suggests that sites penalize people who cash out money from their accounts by giving them bad cards (and/or bad beats). There are even complaints of sites that specialize in particularly brutal bad beats on the river, though

---

[15]Just as I was writing this chapter, PokerStars dealt 1.6 million poker hands in one day. This is more than one of the giant Los Angeles area card barns deals in a month.

[16]And, of course, worry much more than *that* about being hit by a drunk automobile driver.

those theories never seem to get to *why* a site would want to do such a thing.

Another theory says that sites have players, or perhaps bots, playing for the site. These players would get special treatment by the game software, insuring that they win, and thus increasing the site's profits.

Here is the reality of the situation: doing any of the above things is cheating, pure and simple. A site that did any of these would be risking its entire business for a small (probably tiny) increase in rake. And to accomplish that, at least a small handful of people have to know about it. Those people would be potential time-bombs to the site for whom they worked. They could blackmail their employer mercilessly.

But more importantly, it just doesn't make sense. Successful on-line poker sites have a very good, profitable business model. By simply running their business (dealing a fair poker game and keeping their customers happy) they should make a healthy profit. It would be insane to risk that whole thing just for an added percent or two in rake.

The bottom line: if you are interested in playing hold'em online, don't worry about the competence and integrity of the online poker sites. Put your energy into learning to play well and then playing your best game when the chips are down.

Depositing real money

While virtually all poker sites offer "play money" games, those games bear almost no resemblance to poker played for real money. When the price of calling (or raising) is fake chips that you can replenish at will, the game is radically different. So if you're serious about your online poker, you will eventually want to deposit money into an account at one of the online sites and play for real.

Back in the early days of Internet poker, depositing money was as simple as typing in your credit card number, which would be charged for your chips. Then when it got time to cash out, the site would credit the cash-out amount back to your credit card.

Unfortunately, some people used this as a way to defraud the online sites. And eventually the credit card companies got nervous. It has now become quite difficult to find a credit card that can be successfully used for an online poker (or any online gaming) transaction.

The most efficient and easiest way to get money in and out of an online poker account is via an "online wallet" service.[17] You sign up for an account at one of these services, and associate it with an account at your bank or credit union. To deposit $500 into PokerStars, you simply log into your online wallet website, and transfer $500 from your checking account to the online wallet. It may take a day or three to transfer the funds into your online account, so plan accordingly. Then you log into PokerStars, click on the "Buy Chips" button in the cashier, and select your particular online wallet service (like most online sites, PokerStars provides a number of options for depositing funds). You indicate that you want to purchase $500 in chips. The money is transferred from your online wallet into your PokerStars account (in just a few seconds), and you're ready to play.

Now suppose you play well, catch some cards, and run that $500 up to $1500. You decide to withdraw $400. You go back to the PokerStars cashier, and select "Cash Out." You say that you want to cash out $400, and the money is transferred back to your online wallet service. You can now leave it there, send it to another online poker site, or transfer it back into your checking account.

Strategy changes for online play

I discussed various strategy changes for online play throughout the earlier portions of the text, but it's worth reviewing them here.

---

[17]PayPal™ is the best known of these services, but they have chosen to not handle online gaming transactions.

As I discussed above, the anonymity of the Internet takes much of the shame out of playing poorly, so people tend to follow their own instincts and desires. That almost always translates to:

1. More calling.

2. More betting.

3. More raising.

And you should adjust your play accordingly. For instance, you are just about guaranteed a check-raise when you need one. Suppose you flop top-pair top-kicker, but are out of position. You might well want to check-raise to thin the field. The problem, of course, is that you hate to give a free card. Don't worry too much about that online. If it gets around to the button and nobody has bet, very few players seem able to simply take the free card. They bet, and you get your check-raise in.

Conversely, don't be guilty of this yourself. If you're on the button, it's checked around to you, and you need a free card, take it. We discussed that earlier, but it's even more true online. There are two reasons for this. The first is that because there are more callers, the chances of your winning the pot with your bet right there are extremely small. Second, savvy Internet players (such as you are, now) know that few flops ever check around completely. So a clever player may be waiting to spring his check-raise on you. Disappoint him.

Because calling stations are even more frequent than they are in brick and mortar games, play a more straightforward, "honest" game. Bet and raise your good hands, check and fold your bad ones. Bluff rarely. At least in the current "wild west" days of hold'em on the Internet, you'll find this to be a rare playing style. You will see amazing, creative moves that will astound you. And occasionally they'll be successful. But just as happened in California in the late 80's and early 90's, this hyper-aggressive style of play will ultimately fail, and most of its practitioners will go broke and disappear. Do not fall victim to this temptation; simply play your honest game and wait for the cards to fall your way.

Final thoughts

I need to repeat the disclaimer that I put at the beginning of this chapter. I have the uneasy sense of a man describing in detail what he sees at the beach's edge right before the tide comes in. What I write now, I believe to be true. And I expect most of it to be true for at least a couple more years. But I am not so naïve as to think that I can predict what will happen to Internet poker five years from now any better than the soothsayers did five years ago. And nobody that I know predicted what actually happened.

But at this moment in time, Internet poker is great place to learn the game, and play for tiny stakes if you wish. It's a wonderful venue for the elderly, the single parent, the player who lives hundreds of miles from a casino. And it is a gold mine for the expert (or professional) player who wants to maximize his expectation per hour, while having the flexibility to live pretty much anywhere in the world he wishes.

In short, online poker has huge benefits for millions of people. At least for the foreseeable future, it's here to stay.

The No-Limit Sit-and-Go: Introduction

This is the first of three chapters devoted to the no-limit "sit-and-go" tournament.[1] The first chapter gives you an introduction to the form, and some basic groundwork that lets you shift paradigms from limit cash hold'em to a no-limit tournament. The second chapter is the heavy material — the actual strategy. The third chapter is some miscellaneous thoughts on the subject and nuances of play. Finally, in the tradition of this book, is a quiz.

Before I go further, I need to thank my friend and former colleague Terrence Chan. Terrence carefully reviewed and edited this chapter. And many of the points that he added were crucial to the clarity (and indeed, correctness) of this material.

The "sit-and-go" is a unique tournament format that was originally created by online poker sites as an adaptation of the wildly popular single table satellites at major tournaments. The sit-and-go is a 1-3 table tournament, but instead of awarding a single seat in some target event to the last person left, the cash prize pool is distributed among the last 3-5 players. The event is called a "sit-and-go" because it doesn't have a scheduled start time; when there is a player in each seat, cards go into the air.

Now you might reasonably ask why a book about limit cash hold'em games has a chapter about a no-limit tournament

---

[1]I use the term "sit-and-go" rather than the more common "S&G" or "sit & go" just because those terms feel a bit colloquial for this text.

hold'em format.[2] There are two short and powerful answers: "fun" and "profit." Many people find no-limit hold'em to be a more interesting form of poker. If nothing else, it has the adrenaline-pumping opportunity to push all your chips forward and say, "I'm all-in." But more importantly (from my perspective), you may be able to make more money per hour than you can at limit cash hold'em, given a fixed bankroll.[3] I will discuss that in detail later.

Please note: I have placed this chapter toward the back of the book for a reason. I've covered many concepts elsewhere that you need to understand for this section to make sense. If you are brand new to hold'em, please first go read and understand the rest of the book up to this point. Ah, you're back — let us continue.

How no-limit hold'em works

A few years ago, no-limit hold'em was all but dead outside of the major tournaments. TV has changed all that. People who, two years ago, didn't know how many cards there were in the deck can now quote you the odds of QQ vs. AKs all-in.[4] But in the interest of completeness, I'll do a quick review.

No-limit hold'em is usually played with two blinds, just as in limit. However, the terminology of the game is different. If you hear that a limit hold'em game is a $3-6, then you know that the first two rounds of betting are $3 bets and raises, and the last two rounds are $6 bets and raises. In no-limit, the numbers you hear describe the size of the *blinds*. So a $3-6 no-limit game has a small blind of $3 and a big blind of $6. A player acting after the

---

[2]A sit-and-go can be (and they are) played using any poker game and any betting format (limit, pot-limit, and no-limit). However, at this writing, no-limit hold'em is by *far* the most popular form.

[3]My publisher, Conjelco, occasionally publishes a newsletter called the *Intelligent Gambler*. Issue #9 (Summer 1998) contains an extraordinary analysis by J.P. Massar indicating that single table satellites can be more profitable than ring games, with lower variance. The percentage payoff nature of the sit-and-go (multiple players receiving some cash) should further reduce that variance.

[4]53:47 in favor of the queens if they don't contain a card of the opposing suit.

blinds may call the $6 (unless there's been a raise, of course), or raise any amount he wishes, up to the number of chips he has in front of him — thus the "no-limit." The exciting term "all-in" means that he is betting, calling, or raising all of his chips. Unless a player is going all-in, any raise must be at least as large as the last bet or raise during that betting round. So for instance, in a $3-6 no-limit hold'em game (or during the 3-6 blind level of a no-limit hold'em tournament), a player may not raise four chips unless those are his last four chips.

On the flop, turn, and river, any bet must be as large as the big blind, again unless it's an all-in bet. Just as in limit hold'em, a player may check if there's been no bet.

Table stakes and side pots

While all-ins and side pots are relatively rare in limit cash games, they are the bread and butter of no-limit hold'em tournaments. You need to understand them before you get involved in any kind of tournament.

Two fundamental rules will help guide you:

A player may win, from any one opponent, no more chips than he has in front of him at the beginning of the hand.

A player may not be forced out of a pot because he doesn't have enough chips to call a bet or raise.

If you're new to these concepts, I encourage you to wade through the entire example below. It's tedious and time-consuming. You may even want to have little stacks of chips that you move around (you can make each chip count as "50"). But the underlying principles here can dramatically affect correct tournament strategy and you need to understand them.

Suppose you start a hand with 100 chips, your opponent Anne has 250 chips, and Bob has 450 chips. You may go all-in for your 100 chips. If either just Anne *or* Bob calls, then there can be no more betting. Suppose just Anne calls. Then she still has 150 chips left, and you can't win them, because you started with only 100 chips. The board will be dealt out to the river. If you win, then you collect 100 chips from Anne, giving you 200 and she has 150 left. If Anne wins, then she has 350 chips and you are busted out of the tournament.

Now, suppose you go all-in for your 100 chips, Anne calls, and then Bob calls. Anne and Bob each have chips left so the hand proceeds normally; they can still bet and raise. However, your 100 chips plus 100 chips from each of them go into the "main" (or "center") pot. You can win those (along with whatever was in the pot before you made your all-in bet). When the showdown takes place, you must beat all remaining players. If you do, then you win the main pot. Otherwise you will be out of the tournament.

But before this happens, Anne and Bob must complete playing the hand out. At this point, Anne has 150 chips left and Bob has 350. If Anne goes all-in, then Bob would have to call 150 of his remaining 350 chips. Conversely, if Bob goes all-in (or bets any amount 150 or more), then Anne would have to call all 150 of her chips, putting herself all-in. Bob's remaining 200 chips (which Anne can't match) are returned to him. If Anne wins that showdown, then she has 300 chips and Bob has 200. If Bob wins, then he has 500 chips and Anne is busted out.

Let's assume that Bob and Anne go all-in against each other, and that Bob wins (busting out Anne). Then his hand is compared to yours (you've been on the sidelines for the rest of the hand, waiting to see the outcome of Anne and Bob's battle). If he beats your hand, then you bust out as well.[5] However, if your hand beats his, then you win the main pot.

Now, suppose, with you all-in, that Anne bets 50 and Bob calls that. Those 100 chips (50 from each of them) are put into a "side pot" in which you have no interest. Either Anne or Bob can win

---

[5]There is an important point of tournament protocol here. If Bob busts you and Anne on the same hand, then Anne will finish *ahead* of you in the tournament because she started the hand with more chips. For instance, if you are the last three people in the tournament, then Anne would finish in 2nd place and you in 3rd. The difference could be thousands (or tens of thousands) of dollars.

the side pot; you can't. Now there is a 100 chip side pot. On the next card, Anne goes all-in for her remaining 100 chips, but Bob folds. He is giving up interest in not only the side pot with Anne, but the main pot with you as well (this is important). Anne automatically wins the 100 chip side pot, and the remaining board cards (if any) are dealt out. Now you compare your hand against Anne. If you win, fine, you win the main pot. If not, then you're busted out. Note, for example, that if Anne bluffs Bob off the side pot, that is a huge victory for you since now you only have to beat Anne's bluff to win the main pot (and stay in the tournament).

Once you understand the examples above, you'll have the foundation required to make sense of any all-in situations that may come up. But the correct strategy and tactics associated with those are an advanced topic that I won't go into here.

How a sit-and-go works

A sit-and-go tournament is just like a regular tournament, except in scale. Players start with relatively short stack sizes compared to the initial blinds. For instance, you might get 1500 chips with initial blinds of 10 and 20, or 1000 chips with initial blinds of 5 and 10. Then like any tournament, the blinds go up every fixed number of minutes. However, at some sites the blinds increase after a fixed number of hands (generally ten).

If the sit-and-go is one table, then the last three players receive some money. PokerStars has nine-player sit-and-go events, paying 4.5, 2.7, and 1.8 buy-ins to first through third places. For instance, in a $10 sit-and-go, first place gets $45, second gets $27, and third place receives $18. Many other sites have ten-player sit-and-go events, paying 5, 3, and 2 buy-ins to the final three players. For two-table events, four places are paid, and three-table events pay five places.

The fee structure for a sit-and-go is generally about 10% of the buy-in. So a $30 sit-and-go usually has a fee (the house's rake) of $3. That percentage goes down for the larger events, with $15 being a typical fee for a $200 sit-and-go.

The No-Limit Sit-and-Go: Strategy

I am going to repeat this concept over and over throughout this chapter, so I might as well get started here:

Patience is the key to sit-and-go success.[1]

We are still in early years of sit-and-go tournaments. Nobody has been playing them for more than a handful of years (compared to the decades of experience that some professionals have with other hold'em formats). And as I write this, a huge majority of the players have been playing them for less than a year. This means that most people are playing by the seat of their pants. Folks generally play too loosely even when they've read a book or have been around the game awhile. When they're new to the format (and have been getting their lessons from the repeated all-in confrontations on TV), the degree to which they play too many hands too far is shocking.

The way to exploit this behavior is fairly straightforward. First, wait them out. As I state in the main body of this book, they are going to make big mistakes; you rarely need to capitalize on their small ones. The second half of this plan: when you have a monster hand, punish them severely with it (which is capitalizing on their big mistakes).

---

[1] I am reminded of my obsession about telling my scuba students a few dozen times to never hold their breath underwater. While the penalties for erring in a sit-and-go are much less severe, the same principle applies. It's difficult to overstate this point.

Here is an important example: the "TV player" has learned his style from watching nothing but the final tables of major tournaments, and only the most exciting hands of those. He believes that the path to success is non-stop unalloyed aggression. You have a TV player at your table, and at the first blind level, he has jammed the pot (raised all-in) three straight times. On the fourth pot he does it again and you have 33. Your pocket pair is almost certainly a favorite over the two random cards he has. For instance, if he has K9o (which he may consider a monster), then you're about a 6:5 favorite. Don't even consider calling here. Even ignoring the fact that he might have 88 (in which case you're a 4:1 dog), you don't want to do a 6:5 coin flip for all your chips early in the tournament. At some point, it's likely that same guy (or somebody like him) will get all his money in against you when you are a 2:1 (or even bigger) favorite. So there is no point to be "gambling" this early.

Consider, finally, a statement made famous by David Sklansky: if you exactly maintain your chip stack throughout the tournament, you will finish *second*. More frequently than you expect, you will be able to quietly sneak into the money as the other players bash into each other, leaving just one or two monster stacks. You must have a very good excuse to participate in this fray anywhere but toward the end of the tournament.

The importance of implied odds

As important as implied odds are in limit hold'em, they are even more so in no-limit.[2] Your (or your opponent's) entire stack can be at risk on the next bet; you must constantly be mindful of that. First, find opportunities where your opponents are offering you good implied odds. Second, try not to offer them to your opponents. A classic example of getting good implied odds is calling a small percentage of your stack before the flop with a pocket pair. As a rule of thumb, call before the flop in middle or late position with *any* pocket pair if you can do so for no more than 7%

---

[2] If you haven't read the subsection "Implied odds" beginning on page 34, please do so before continuing here.

of the chips you can win.[3] The reason is that many (perhaps most) players are willing to commit their entire stacks with top pair on the flop. If you flop a set, you may well get an opponent to commit all his chips drawing very nearly dead.

Another example of this is calling a bet with a gutshot straight draw, even if the pot is not nearly big enough to justify the call. For instance, suppose you have JT and the flop is K-8-7 rainbow. It's fine to call up to about 5% of the money that you can win, given your 11:1 odds of hitting the nuts with a nine on the turn.[4] In this situation, you don't care as much about the current size of the pot; your sights are on your opponent's entire stack.

The other side of the coin is to avoid giving your opponents good implied odds. Specifically, you need to bet enough that your opponents aren't getting the right implied odds against *you*. For instance, a good initial pre-flop raise should be about three times the big blind. This prevents other players (and particularly the big blind) from calling just for nuisance purposes.

Or suppose you raise with AK and get a great flop: K-7-3. You should bet at least 2/3 to 3/4 of the pot at this point. If you have put in a decent raise before the flop, then a minimum bet (the size of the big blind) will offer a very good price to somebody with 87, based on the current pot size alone (not to mention implied odds). If he hits an 8 or 7 on the turn (neither a particularly threatening card), then he may be able to win all your chips from you, or make a big bet, forcing *you* to fold. If he calls a bet of more than half the pot, he's generally making a mathematical mistake.

---

[3]Note that I said "chips you can win," and not "your chips." Remember that the opposing players' stacks that you intend to win must be big enough to justify the call, as well as your own.

[4]If you have KQ and the flop is J-9-2, you might be willing to call a few more of your chips because a king or queen could easily give you the best hand (along with a ten giving you the nuts). But do *not* call on the strength of overcards alone.

Position

I spent a fair amount of time in the main portions of this text lecturing about position. But it's important to discuss here because the stakes are even higher. When the next bet can put somebody all-in, the opportunity to act last is extraordinarily important. Furthermore, you live in less fear of the check-raise.

Check-raising is not as important in no-limit hold'em because (1) it can be so catastrophic to give a free card and (2) because you don't need it to force your opponents into a bad call. For instance, suppose you have flopped top pair with a good kicker in a limit hold'em game. But there are a couple of possible gutshot draws on the board, and you're out of position against three other players. A check-raise is a very reasonable play since if the last player bets, you can force the middle two players to pay two bets for their four- or five-out draws. In a no-limit game, you don't need this finesse. You just put in a bet of 2/3 or 3/4 the size of the pot. Now your opponents are almost certainly making a bad call if they have 4-5 outs. Note also that if you attempt a check-raise and it fails, you have given a free card that could cost you not only the pot but perhaps many more chips. If one of your opponents hits a second pair or a gutshot straight, you're unlikely to recognize it, and may end up getting busted.

Given that the check-raise is both less necessary and more dangerous in no-limit hold'em, position is that much more powerful.

Also, get out of any habits that you have of over-defending your blinds.[5] A player who makes a good raise will not offer you the 3:1 odds that you get in a limit game. If you have a hand that demands to be played, then play it, but seriously consider re-raising and betting the flop; just rip control from your opponent. Players who call too many raises on their blinds are doomed to failure in the sit-and-go world.

Of course, if a raiser makes a silly one-big-blind raise and gets a caller or three, then you can call with speculative hands such as suited connectors — you're getting the right price and right im-

---

[5]I assure you, you didn't learn them in this book.

plied odds. But you'd often rather call a small raise cold on the button than that same raise on the big blind.

Fold equity

Many players don't seem to understand this important concept; be sure that you do:

It's much better to bet or raise than call.

And the reason for this is simple: there's a good chance that your opponents will *fold*, and you don't have to go any further in the hand. You almost always have higher expected value by winning the dead money[6] in the pot with a bet (or raise) than having a showdown. That's because you have zero risk of losing the pot if your opponents all fold. That extra expectation you gain by avoiding a showdown is called "fold equity."

Avoid crippling bets, raises, and calls

When you're playing a limit cash game, you don't have to worry about your stack size very much. Simply by rebuying when necessary, you can always have enough chips to handle all the betting that can take place during a single hand. But in tournaments, and particularly no-limit tournaments, you don't have that luxury — you need to be aware of your and your opponents' stack sizes at all times.

A main reason for this is to insure that your bets and raises don't leave you crippled and "pot-committed." For example, suppose the blinds are 50-100 and you have 400 chips. You are the first person into the pot and you have two nines. A normal opening raise would be 275-300 chips. But a 300 chip raise would leave you with only 100 chips. If your pre-flop raise is called, then there will be at least 650 chips in the pot. You will have to put the last 100 chips into the pot on the flop anyway — you'll be getting 6.5:1 odds, and the 99 is almost always at least that good. Therefore, you should simply push all-in for your last 400 chips before the flop. You're hoping that nobody will call anyway (fold equi-

---

[6]Anything that's in the pot before you make your bet or raise.

ty), so make it as unpleasant as possible for your opponents to call.

Or, suppose you're the table bully with 3000 chips and five players left. The blinds are 100-200, and the big blind has 600 chips after posting his blind. You have 88 — definitely a raising hand in this situation. A normal raise (three times the big blind) would be 600 chips. But if you raise to 800, you force the big blind to play for all of his chips. Don't give him the option of calling your raise and then folding on the flop, with 200 chips to get through another orbit of the button. Furthermore, with your particular hand, you'd be delighted to win the blinds without a fight, and the extra 200 chips in your raise may deter the opposition.

Early stage

Let's call the first three blind levels of the sit-and-go the early stage. On PokerStars, for instance, that would be through the 25-50 blind levels. And probably only one or two players will bust out during those first three rounds.

Note also that this is where the most "poker" is played after the flop. As the average stack:blind ratio decreases,[7] many hands will essentially play themselves.

You will be largely uninvolved during this stage of the tournament unless you happen to pick up a big hand. The only raising hands you play are: AA-TT, AKs, AKo, AQs, AQo.

With those big hands, you should raise approximately three times the big blind if you're the first person in. If there is a caller or two, raise a bit more, perhaps "three plus the number of callers" times the big blind. You are adjusting your raise to reduce the pot odds being offered to anybody to call.

If there has been a raise in front of you, you should re-raise to about three times the amount of the original raise. For instance, suppose the blinds are 15-30, and somebody makes it 100 to go (that is, raises *to* 100). With JJ, you should re-raise to about 300.[8]

---

[7]That is, the blinds will begin to represent an increasing percentage of the average stack size. As this happens, you will see more all-in confrontations, and they will come earlier in the hand.

Especially if you're putting in a re-raise, and unless you have AA or KK, it would be nice if the hand ended right there. But it probably won't.

If you flop top pair or an overpair (or better), then you will have to commit all your chips given the opportunity. As is generally the case with no-limit hold'em, this assumes that you have a single opponent. Obviously, the more opponents you have, the more you should be willing to abandon just a single pair to a large bet.

But fundamentally, if you have a single opponent and have made top pair or better, then you bet (or raise) on the flop. And you bet again on the turn, unless it's a terrifying card for you. *Most* of the time, you're going to win the pot at some point during that sequence.

As an example, early in the tournament, you have the starting stack of 1500 chips and the blinds are 10-20. You get Q♥-Q♣. One player calls before it gets to you. You raise to 70. It's folded back around to the caller, who calls your raise. The flop comes T♠-8♠-3♥. He checks. The pot is 170. A good bet would be about 130. That is big enough to prevent his making an easy call with something like 9♥-8♥.

If he calls and checks again on the turn, you should bet again. If you had bet 130 on the flop and were called, then the pot will be 430 on the turn. A good bet there would be about 300. Notice that I didn't even discuss what the turn card was — you should be betting pretty much regardless of what it is.

If he calls and checks again on the river, you can check as well; you've gotten very good value with your single pair.

Going back to the flop, if your opponent bets, you should raise. If he makes a solid bet (as you would) of 130 chips, raise about three times his bet, perhaps to a total of 500. That does two things:

---

[8]Noting, for the last time, that you must always keep in mind the effect of these plays on your and your opponents' stacks. For instance, if the original raiser has 275 chips left after his raise, you should re-raise enough to put him all-in.

1. It crushes any odds he's hoping to get for a big draw (such as a flush draw). Remember, this isn't limit hold'em. He's faced with having to call another, bigger bet on the turn. He only gets one card for this call, and he's not getting the right price for it.

2. It sets up the pot size so you can get the rest of your chips into the pot on the turn. If he calls the 500 chips on the flop, then on the turn, there will be 1170 chips in the pot, and you'll have 930 left (you bet 70 pre-flop, and 500 on the flop).

Of course, your opponents don't have to play correctly. In fact, they probably won't, nor do you want them to. Sometimes, your opponent will make a bad call of those 500 chips, hit his flush on the turn, and bust you. But when he is paying 1/3 of his chips to chase a 4:1 draw for a single card, you are gaining expected value and he is losing it.

The same thing is true on the turn. Suppose the turn misses your opponent's draw, but he calls your all-in bet with his flush draw. He is getting only a hair better than 2:1 on his call, yet is again a 4:1 dog to hit the flush on the river.

If your opponent has a different draw (e.g., AT or J9), then he is making an even worse mathematical mistake by calling your bets, as he has fewer outs.

Suited aces and connectors

Notice that while I mention sneaking into pots with small pocket pairs, I didn't say anything about suited aces and connectors — hands such as A6s and 98s. That's because playing small pairs is fairly straightforward: you flop a set or you don't. If you don't, you get out. If you do, you try to get all your money in. But note that you make your hand (or don't) *on the flop*. A suited ace (or any two suited cards) will flop a four-flush with about the same probability as a pair flopping a set (once every eight times). But when you flop a draw, you still have to hit one of your outs. In a limit game, you can almost always get the necessary odds to do that. But a strong no-limit player isn't going to let you draw cheaply. If he plays as I suggest in this chapter, he's going to be betting over half the pot, and you aren't getting the right price to chase. As I said in the introduction, players who chase draws in no-limit without getting the right odds are destined for a short and/or expensive career.

The other danger of suited aces is that you'll flop a pair of aces with a bad kicker and get tied to it. While this is a bad idea in limit hold'em, it can be fatal in no-limit. Avoiding those kinds of hands avoids those kinds of mistakes.

With that said, though, there are some circumstances in which you can play suited aces and connectors. First, you must be in good position relative to the button. Any hand that is this awkward to play needs to have everything else going for it. Second, you want to play this hand in a pot against weak minimum-betting, free-card-giving players. The kind of players who will let you draw at your straight or flush for a reasonable price (or no price at all).

Once in a *great* while, you can semi-bluff on the flop with a flush draw (or even better, a 15-out straight-flush-ish draw). If you're going to do this, you should make a big raise or move all-in. This guarantees that you'll get two cards if your opponent calls. And it prevents your opponent from re-raising and forcing you out of the pot.

Finally, don't call with unsuited connectors — they're just more trouble than they're worth.

Getting re-raised pre-flop

Sometimes you make a normal pre-flop raise and an opponent re-raises you. You have two obvious factors to consider when deciding what to do next: your cards, and the size of his re-raise.

If you have AA-QQ, you'd like to get all the chips in, either now or on the flop. Regardless of the size of his re-raise, put in a large re-raise. For instance, suppose the blinds are 15-30, you have 1400 chips, there are two callers, and then you make it 120 (a very reasonable raise). Now your opponent makes a substantial re-raise, say to 350. You should re-raise to 900-1000 chips, with the intent of putting the rest of them in on the flop. Of course if your opponent re-raises all-in (or puts you all-in) then you call without hesitation.

Now suppose, instead, that your opponent puts in a piddling re-raise — perhaps even the minimum amount (90 chips), making it 210 to go. You should raise to about 500. If he calls that, then again, you can move in on the flop with your remaining 900 chips. The only thing that should stop you from doing this would be a card on the flop higher than your big pair.

If you are re-raised pre-flop holding two big cards (AK being the prime example) or JJ-TT, then you should *not* be looking for an all-in showdown immediately.[9] Consider the same scenario as the last one (big blind is 30, there are two callers, and you have 1400 chips). You make the same raise to 100, and are re-raised. Of course, you're much less happy to be re-raised holding AK than KK. If the re-raise is not more than 200-300 additional chips, you should call.

If you flop top pair (or an overpair), then assume you have best hand and play accordingly. If you don't flop top pair, you might take a shot at the pot if there is some hand you could credibly hold (perhaps you have AQs and the flop is king-high). But if you do that, then you have to bet the same amount you'd bet if you'd hit the flop square on. Or if you have TT and the flop is J-7-3, you should seriously consider betting. But you must be *much* more careful than you'd be if the flop were 9-7-3.

Otherwise, you pretty much have to check and fold. Remember, there is no shame in checking and folding; don't feel obliged to hopelessly bluff your chips away.

One final point concerning early stage strategy: if you make a reasonable raise (or even re-raise) pre-flop with AK and an opponent moves all-in for a lot of chips, you should fold without hesitation. It is possible that you have a dominating hand (e.g.,

---

[9]Remember, this is in the early stages of the sit-and-go. Toward the end of the event, AQ and TT are hands with which you get all-in.

your opponent has KQ or AQ), but you may very well find yourself in a coin flip (against a medium pair). If your opponent has two smaller cards but they're "live" (that is, you have neither of those ranks), you are only about a 3:2 favorite. There is no reason to make these gambles early on.

When an opponent suddenly springs to life

The previous discussion assumes that your opponents are playing along nicely. If they fold, great. And if they call, you have a plan. But suppose an opponent suddenly becomes aggressive. For instance, you get check-raised on the flop, or your opponent checks and calls on the flop, but bets out on the turn.

A few players use this unexpected play as a bluff, and you should note who they are. But usually this sequence means that your opponent has a strong hand.

This brings us to a very interesting discussion: what is a "strong" hand? Because strong is only meaningful in comparison to another hand. Remember, ace-high beats king-high just as surely as a straight flush beats one pair. When you're playing limit hold'em, and there are more people involved further into the hand, the average hand you need to win is higher than if only two people saw the flop. And two people seeing the flop is much more common in a no-limit hold'em sit-and-go than it is in a limit hold'em cash game.

My point here is that your opponent may decide that he has a strong hand, but your hand is still stronger. Remember, you are only playing premium hands; you are far more selective than most of your opponents are. The best example is your flopping an overpair. Most players consider top pair to be a huge hand, and don't give much credence to the possibility of a larger pair. So they may make a scary move on you (thinking they have the best hand) when in fact they are drawing at only five outs.

Therefore, you will often have to commit yourself even though your opponent's language (via his bets) is that he can beat you. For instance, suppose the blinds are 25-50, you have 1200 of your original 1500 chips, and you raise to 150 with K♠-K♦. You get one caller (who has more chips than you), and the flop comes Q♥-9♣-2♥. Your opponent checks, you bet 250, and he check-raises to 600. You should jam (move all-in) without hesitation. This is a situation known as "having more than you promised." That is, your opponent expects you to bet a large range of hands — KQ, any two hearts, JJ, A♥-K♦, and so on. So if he has AQ (or even A9), he might well think he has the best hand. Furthermore, you don't want to let him successfully semi-bluff with a heart draw or JT.

Occasionally, you've announced real strength in your hand, but your opponent keeps charging. For instance, you have AK, have raised, and the flop is A-7-8 rainbow. Your opponent bets, you raise, and he calls. Now the turn is a jack. He checks, you bet, and he check-raises you. If your opponent's reputation is for squeaky tight and uncreative play, you are almost certainly beaten. Now the only question is whether you're getting sufficient pot odds that you're forced to call. Note that if he has AJ, you have three outs. If he has A7, you have nine outs. At the extremes, if he has T9 or a set, then you're drawing dead, but if he has AQ, then *he* has only three outs.

But absent other information, you need to call most of the time for the following reasons:

1. You usually "have more than you promised." Your opponent may well believe he has the best hand, but be wrong.

2. Even if you're behind, you're often drawing at a healthy number of outs. Given that you may be in front and if not, have outs, calling can't be terribly wrong.

3. You don't want to give the impression that you can be moved off of a hand easily. You don't play very many hands, so when you do play one, you need to strongly commit to it.

You flop a monster

While this is rare, it's worth discussing, because these are the situations where you plan to get yourself (or an opponent) all-in.

Most often, this will be a set that you've flopped. But occasionally you'll flop the miracle straight or flush.

In general, you would like to get all the money in on the flop. Failing that, you want to make sure that your opponent is making a mathematical mistake by calling a bet or raise that you make. Specifically, assume for the moment that you have the best hand, and ask yourself what hand(s) are you most worried about facing. Given that an opponent holds the most dangerous of those hands, make sure that he isn't getting the right odds (true or implied) to catch a card and bust you.

For instance, suppose you have J♣-J♦, and have put in a normal raise before the flop, which comes J♠-9♥-2♥. While you obviously have the nuts at the moment, a hand like QT or A♥-8♥ is drawing quite heavily against you. The worst situation you could be in is that your opponent has Q♥-T♥ (a straight-flush draw), but first, that's monsters under the bed, and second, you're still a 3:2 favorite against that hand.[10] So, more reasonably, put your opponent on a nine-out flush draw, and bet accordingly. He's about a 4:1 dog to hit his card on the turn, so make sure that you bet at least 25% of the available money on the flop. If he calls that, the dreaded heart comes on the turn, and he pushes all-in, you have a difficult decision. You are about a 7:2 dog if he does have the flush, so if the pot is laying you that price, then you *have* to call. But of course there's a chance he's making a semi-bluff with a hand like A♥-9♣, in which case you're well ahead. So you need to call even if the pot doesn't justify a call against a made flush.

Of course, if he makes a bet that gives you the right odds to draw at filling up, then call. A lot of players don't understand the correct strategy in a situation like this and will bet small, even with a flush, thinking they're "sucking you in." If he lets you fill up cheaply when you could bust him, he's the one making the mistake.

---

[10]Note that if you have more than one or two opponents, it's quite reasonable to assume that both those draws are against you.

If the flush card hits and your opponent checks again (or you're forced to bet first), you should bet most of the time. Particularly if you're checked to, you should bet. Most of the time, a check means what it says ("I'm weak"), and you don't want to give a free card to a singleton heart. Note that if you had something like A♥-J♣, you'd want to check because it's difficult for a worse hand to call you, and you are not particularly afraid of a free card.

If you hit a huge hand with an ace-high or king-high flop, you should be even more aggressive. A lot of players simply can't fold an ace, and will commit all their chips with that top pair. This is exactly the sort of all-in confrontation you're seeking.

Middle stage

Think of the next three levels as the "middle stage." On Poker-Stars, that would be the 50-100 blind level through the 100-200 level. Notice that you won't be doing as much play after the flop because a reasonable raise before the flop and a good sized bet on the flop is likely to get somebody all-in.

Your job here is to maintain your chip position, and perhaps increase it by stealing blinds if you can. Again, avoid all-in confrontations unless you expect to have *much* the best of it (perhaps 3:1 or better).

Unless you have been fortunate to build up a large stack (probably doubling your stack or better), you can't play speculative hands. That means no more limping in with pairs hoping to flop a set — you're just not getting the right price. At the lower end of the range, just dump them. At the higher end of the medium pairs, you may need to raise. If you've got less than five times the sum of the blinds, then it's time to find a hand to play. For instance, suppose the blinds are 75-150 and you have 1000 chips. If you get 77 and are the first person raising, you should jam. Obviously, you hope not to get called (if you do, you're likely no better than a slight favorite). But you'd be delighted to pick up those 225 chips right now. Even better would be if one or two people had called in front of you. Now if you jam and they all fold, you pick up 425 chips — a wonderful profit if you don't have to see a flop for it.

If you have managed to double your stack and are in solid chip position, look for an opportunity during each blind round to steal one set of blinds. Particularly if you can make a standard opening raise without really hurting yourself, this is a good time to get aggressive. Presumably a few people will have busted out at this point, and people are starting to think about making the money. If you can pick up one or two sets of blinds during a single blind level, you increase your stack nicely with virtually no risk. If somebody re-raises you, don't feel obliged to get involved unless you're committed to the pot (usually because the raiser couldn't raise enough to make a fold correct).

Also, don't do anything stupid.[11] This may sound like silly advice, but no-limit hold'em is an unforgiving game. If you're the second chip leader, and the chip leader puts in a big raise, don't get involved with anything but an absolutely premium hand. For instance, suppose he raises with JT and you jam with 88. Assuming you both have lots of chips, he should fold the JT without hesitation. But maybe he doesn't know that. So now the two of you are flipping a 53:47 coin and either you get busted, or he gets almost busted. And everybody else at the table (particularly the third place guy) is ecstatic. Continuing, it is almost certainly a mistake to re-raise with JJ if the chip leader raises, and you're in second place with a large stack. Of course, making an initial raise with JJ, or jamming with it if you're low on chips, is fine. But don't take risks you don't *have* to.

If it's folded to you on the button, raise liberally — A9 or any two cards bigger than a ten, any pair. You're only laying 2:1 to win the blinds, and they're faced with playing out of position against a raiser. Be particularly opportunistic if the big blind is in a marginal but not desperate chip situation (perhaps 4th or 5th stack,

---

[11]Lest you get the wrong impression, I speak here from experience. My hope is that by writing this in the book, I will burn the point into my own poker consciousness.

4-6 times the blinds). He is likely to want to avoid confrontations and hope to sneak into the money.

Late stage and the bubble[12]

Your first job here is *survival*, and that's even if you're the chip leader. In a large multi-table tournament, the payoff curve rises sharply to the final table, and even more sharply at it. Therefore, it may be worth risking busting out if it will put you in a position to win the "real" money. But in a one-table sit-and-go, the biggest payoff jump is going from 4th to 3rd place. As an example at PokerStars, 4th place loses one buy-in, and 3rd place wins 1.8 buy-ins — an advance of 2.8 buy-ins. The step to 2nd place is only another 0.9 buy-ins, and up to 1st is 1.8 buy-ins. Other sites have similar structures. So the most important thing you can do is insure (or reach) 3rd place.[13]

Many players screw down extremely tightly here, but others seem to have no realization of the importance of survival. You must identify these two types of players, because you play very differently against each. Against players who are trying to sneak into the money, steal at every opportunity. Conversely, against players with no survival instinct, only play against them if you have a monster. Realize that if there are two or more such players, they may well manage to take each other out; let them.

If you are in already in the money (by stack position), then look for ways to protect and increase your stack, but without jeopardizing your position. That is, you would like to steal some blinds, but don't try if losing those chips would drop you out of the top three stacks. The only exception would be if there are only one or two players left to act after you, and you "know" that they will fold.

If it's folded to you on the button, put in your standard raise with any ace, any king, QJ, and any pair. Be a bit more conservative

---

[12]The "bubble" is the point at which just a single player must be eliminated before everybody is in the money. It has also become a verb.

[13]Of course, this assumes that you're in a one-table event paying three spots. Adjust accordingly if more players are being paid.

if you've got the button to act behind you. Be a bit more conservative, also, if it's folded to you in the small blind. That's because if you are called, you'll be out of position. For that reason, if it's close between folding and raising, you should fold. And if it's close between a normal raise and moving all-in, prefer moving all-in. Notice I said nothing about calling; don't call.

If you are fortunate enough to have built up a big chip lead (good things occasionally happen to good players), then you should mercilessly pound on the weaker stacks. Do not give them a chance to see a flop cheaply or get a walk in the blinds. And when you go after them, tend to move all-in. You are saying, "If you wish to play your hand, you will be doing so for all your chips. Wouldn't you prefer to have somebody else risk all *his* chips against me?"

If you are not in the top three stacks, then obviously you need to advance. There are three ways you can move up — here they are in order of preference:

1.   Two big stacks clash, busting or crippling one of them.

2.   You steal blinds.

3.   You get into a big confrontation and win it.

Note that the most desirable approach is the one minimizing your exposure to harm. Only if you come up with a monster hand such as KK would you be enthusiastic about an all-in showdown.

Because stealing blinds is more desirable than an all-in showdown, consider fold equity carefully when deciding where to make your move. If somebody has raised in front of you, any re-raise you make will almost surely be called. So re-raising all-in with something like a weak ace is not correct unless you're in desperate chip situation (you have less than three times the sum of the blinds). You would prefer to be the first aggressor with K3 than the previous situation.

In the money

Once you make the money, expect the play to loosen up dramatically. And in some senses, this is correct play, because all of you have leapt the important "bubble" hurdle.

There is likely to be some significant "gambling" going on immediately after the bubble. It may be best to wait for a hand or two and see if somebody self-destructs. Of course, if you pick up a big hand, play it. And remember that with just three players, hand values change dramatically — a pair of 8's is a monster.

Realize that in close-quarters combat like this, hands such as suited connectors have essentially no value. You want cards that have high card or pair value. So 44 is more valuable than 98s. When there are confrontations between two hands, it's usually something like your 33 against his QJ, or your K8 against his A7. And you're hoping to make (or avoid) a single pair; straights and flushes rarely come into play.

If you are the chip leader, pick on the second place stack if possible. He's more likely to give up blinds, letting you increase your lead. It's particularly convenient if you're the chip leader and the other two stacks are roughly equal. Neither will want to get into a confrontation that could let the other sneak into second place.

If you're in second place, then you'd like to steal from the short stack if possible. But don't try to steal from him with a weak hand like 98 if he's sufficiently short-stacked that he's going to feel obliged to call (or raise all-in).

If you're the short stack, it's somewhat like being out of the money near the bubble — you need to move up. Look for a place where you can raise (or jam) with some fold equity. Obviously, the second place stack is your preferred target. Finally, this may be the perfect place for the "stop-and-go" play described in the next chapter. Be aware of it and ready to use it.

Heads-up

Having gotten to the heads-up play (two players left), you now have the opportunity to make the next largest jump in payoff since you got past the bubble. This is not a time for slacking off; give it your best concentration.

Many players do not correctly adjust for the changing hand values as you get down short-handed, and particularly when you are heads-up. Realize that between two random hold'em hands, the winning hand is just a high card 6% of the time. One pair accounts for another 38% of the wins, and two pair for 33%. And some of those one and two pair hands will involve the board pairing (helping neither player).

Usually, the blinds will have reached a point that you have little choice but to jam or fold before the flop. If not, and you think you can outplay your opponent, then you can put in a standard raise before the flop. In a heads-up tournament situation, the button has the small blind and acts first before the flop. So you hope to steal the big blind with your raise, but if not, you have position on your opponent. Conversely, don't make speculative calls on the big blind when you're raised — you'll be out of position against a raiser with an already large pot that's difficult to give up. More often, you should either fold or move all-in.

Given that players are likely to not defend their big blind enough and that you're going to be jamming or folding, what hands should you jam with? Any ace, any king, any pair. Larger queens. Any two cards both higher than eight. If it's clear that your opponent won't defend enough, then raise with almost anything.

Conversely, if you're forced to call all your chips, use the same guidelines as you would for doing the raising yourself. However, if you've got an opponent who is pounding on you, don't let him wear your stack down to the point where you won't be able to get back. If you reach a point where doubling your chips won't get you back to even against your opponent, it's time to make a stand. Pick a hand and go with it. Interestingly, you might prefer to have something like 86 instead of K2 when defending against a raise. If your opponent is raising with KT, your K2 is an 8:3 underdog, but the 86 is only 7:4 behind. Neither of those are particularly *good*, of course, but the difference is meaningful.

If your opponent just calls on the button, you should often jam right there. Usually a call in that position means "I don't particularly like my hand, but I want to see a flop." Don't let him. Every once in a while, you'll discover that he called with KK. Those things happen. But it's a huge win if you can take a full big blind without a showdown when you're out of position and will get the button on the next hand. Another (more dangerous) alternative is to check and then bet the flop no matter what it is. Remember, *most* of the time, neither of you will flop anything, and whoever gets his money in first is likely to win the hand

The No-Limit Sit-and-Go: Miscellaneous

As promised, here are a number of moderately random thoughts about sit-and-go strategy and the whole milieu. I encourage you, however, to carefully read the section about bankroll requirements and profit.

Studying your opponents

No-limit hold'em, much more than limit poker, is about playing your opponents as much as the cards. And the no-limit hold'em sit-and-go is no exception. In a limit game, you can often just shrug your shoulders and pay off a bettor who is representing a better hand than yours. Doing that in a no-limit game will cost you a fortune.

So you must take careful notes; use the online sites' "player note" feature heavily.[1] Suppose you are holding a fairly strong hand, but now a player check-raises your big bet on the turn. Wouldn't it be nice to look at the notes on him and see "Check-raises just for the thrill of it" or "If he check-raises, he has the nuts."

Some of the things to note about your opponents:

1. If he makes a small bet (compared to the pot size), is it a bluff, an attempt to suck people in, or is he simply clueless about how big he should bet?

---

[1] This is where programs such as PokerTracker and PokerOffice truly shine.

2. Does he check-raise, ever? If so, under what circumstances?

3. Is he a calling station — or can you steal blinds from him? Or will he call before the flop, but then routinely fold on the flop?

4. Does he understand the nuances of tournament strategy? Will he fold when it's in his best interest to do so, even if it's in yours too?

5. Will he commit all of his chips with top pair on the flop? With less than top pair?

You get the idea — the more information you have about a player, the easier it will be to make some of the difficult decisions that a no-limit sit-and-go demands.

Feeler bets, bluffs, and minimum bets

Many players don't understand the basic mathematics of no-limit hold'em, which we covered in the previous chapter. The whole point of no-limit is that you can bet any amount you wish, scaling your bet size to the size of the pot, the pot odds you wish to offer (or not), etc.

And yet you routinely see players betting 20 chips into a 200 chip pot, or raising that 20 chip bet to 40 chips. These sorts of bets and raises make no sense — they are giving the other players enormous pot odds (and implied odds) to call and clobber the bettor with the next card off the deck.

First, it should be obvious that you don't want to make bets like this. Whether you are betting "probably" the best hand, the stone cold nuts, or a stone cold bluff, your bets should be in the same general range. Otherwise, your tougher opponents will know which type of hand you have. Not only that, but as we discussed earlier, you don't want to be giving your opponents good pot odds to call your bets.

But since your opponents will be making bets like this, you should understand what those bets mean. Some players scale their bet size very nicely to their perceived value of the hand they hold. Obviously, learn that about them, and use it against them.

Other players put out "feeler" bets — a small (or even minimum) bet into a big pot, designed to see if they get any callers at all. Against such a player, you can occasionally represent the hand he's trying to sniff out. For instance, a third card of a single suit comes on the turn, and a player bets 50 chips into a 400 chip pot. He may be looking to see if anybody has a flush. If you want to put a move on this opponent, either raise immediately, or call his little bet and then raise (or bet) a nice healthy pot-scaled bet on the river. Generally, you'll win the pot right there.

Other players have a tendency to make those same silly little bets as bluffs. Use the same strategy on them — raise and make them play for real; generally they'll just give up quickly.

The exception to this strategy is when you have a big drawing hand. There is no reason to risk a re-raise when you really would like to see the next card. If an opponent is foolish enough to offer you 5:1 or 10:1 on a good draw, take it and don't risk being blown out of the pot by a big re-raise.

Calling a big bet on the flop with AK (no pair)

Don't.

The stop-and-go

Suppose you have 1200 chips, are the short stack, the sit-and-go is on the bubble, and you must post a big blind of 300 chips. It is folded to the button, who makes a minimum raise to 600. The small blind folds. You have 99 — what should you do? Clearly you're going to play; under the circumstances, you have a huge hand. But suppose your opponent has AK (or any two over-cards). You're probably well aware that your pocket nines are just a tiny favorite against the overcards. And if you jam at this point, he will surely call.

The correct play is often to *call* the raise and then promptly shove your chips in on the flop, *without looking*. That is, you move all-in, regardless of what cards come. Of course, if he flopped top pair (or perhaps any pair) then he will quickly call, and unless you hit a set, you'll be busted. But that would have happened if you had jammed before the flop.

However, suppose the flop misses him, and now you push all-in? It may well be correct for him to call anyway, but many players won't recognize this. And it's a much thinner call now that the flop is out of the way and there are just two cards left to hit his six outs. You may well get your opponent to fold in this situation, not only saving you the agony of that dreaded pair card hitting on the river, but nicely padding your chip stack too.

This play was first discussed (to my knowledge) by David Sklansky, and it has gotten some publicity from 2004 World Series of Poker champion, Greg Raymer. It is a powerful addition to your arsenal. It is also a powerful weapon in your opponents' hands. Be sure not to make raises that will allow your opponent to free roll you with a stop-and-go.[2]

The re-steal jam

The stock market has a theory called "the greater fool." The idea is that you can buy a stock, no matter how overvalued, and still make a profit as long as you can find a "greater fool" to buy it from you at a still higher price. A similar situation can take place in a sit-and-go.

Suppose you are down to four players, one away from the money. There is one player who is significantly worse off than the other three; you have every expectation that this person will "bubble," putting the rest of you in the money. You are on the big blind, and it's folded to the small blind; both of you have healthy stacks. Now the small blind makes a standard raise. In some senses, he is already doing something a little foolish. Nobody (except the short stack) should be risking a great deal at this point; they should all wait for the last place guy to bust out so they're in the money. But the small blind may be thinking a similar thing about you: "If I raise here, the big blind won't want to

---

[2]If you spot somebody using this play, make a note about him; he is a player to be reckoned with.

get involved; he knows better. So he will fold almost automatically. He does not want to be a bigger fool than I am."

Now, sometimes you can make the following play: when somebody raises you in that situation, re-raise him *all-in*. You have changed the situation completely: you have shown yourself to be a greater fool than he, but by jamming, you've made it impossible for him to re-raise. Now his only options are to call or fold. If he calls, then he's making fools of *both* of you (to the delight of the tiny stack).

Obviously, you'd like him to fold rather than call your insane re-raise. Therefore, to make this play, you need your opponent to be aware of the dynamics of the situation, or at least to have a healthy fear of all-in confrontations on the bubble. Also, your opponent must not have an ego problem that prevents him from being the person to back down in this clash of fools. But if those two conditions hold, this play can collect you a pile of chips while avoiding the dreaded all-in.

Don't count on your opponent to help

Tournament poker creates unusual situations in which you are counting on a different kind of "implicit collusion" than is described elsewhere in this text. Consider this common occurrence at the end of a sit-and-go: the tournament is down to three players; player A goes all-in, and players B and C blithely check right to the showdown without a pause. Their intent is to insure that the better of their two hands is around to (hopefully) bust out A and guarantee each of them one higher step up the payoff ladder. While this is not always the correct strategy, it gives you an idea of the odd alliances that exist toward the end of a poker tournament.

In the previous section, I describe a scenario where you move all-in, trusting that your opponent won't risk a fatal confrontation with you when there's a player almost out of chips.

You can't always count on your opponents to play along.

In fact, I might say that you can *rarely* count on your opponents to play along. Many players simply don't understand the mathematics of such situations. Even if they do, their egos get the better of them. They get tired of your raising them out of the pot, though they know that they should promptly fold to your raise (with a crippled opponent watching expectantly on the sidelines).

Be slow to give your opponents credit for the understanding and cool to avoid a potentially fatal confrontation with you. You may be betting your survival in the tournament on your opponent's cleverness when such a bet is both unnecessary and poorly made.

Scooping up the limpers

Sometimes a bunch of people will try to limp in to see a flop. Occasionally you can put in a big raise and win all that "dead" money without seeing a flop.

If you're going to make this play, you have to put in a big enough raise that nobody will want to call you. As a rule of thumb, treat it just as you would a normal opening raise: add three to the number of callers and make the raise that many times the big blind. For instance, if the big blind is 30 chips and there are five callers, then 5+3=8, so raise to 240. Note that this is a huge raise for a 30 chip big blind, but you want it to be; you don't want anybody calling. Of course, people will suspect that you're doing exactly what you are doing, but often none of them will be willing to be the one to stop you.

Sklansky discusses this play as well, but suggests that you make it with a hand that's a complete bluff. His point is that if you make this with a hand that would like to see a flop (such as AJs or 99) and you're re-raised, you'll have to throw your hand away. And you hate that because if you'd just limped in like everybody else, you could have seen a flop cheaply.

However, I think that the current sit-and-go world is different for an important reason: you are much more likely to get *called* somewhere than re-raised. So you'd like to have a hand that has a chance of hitting the flop reasonably if you're called. That is, you don't need to have a normal raising hand, but don't do it with trash. Hands like the AJs or 99 that Sklansky was afraid of seem like exactly the right hands with which to make this play.

Also, Sklansky suggested making this play on the big blind. I think in this world, it's best to make it when you have position, in case you *are* called. Now you don't feel quite so miserable about playing on the flop if you must.

Of course, be aware of the player who has this play in his book. Don't try to limp in with a bunch of people if he's to act behind you because he may raise a lot and force you out. Conversely, you may be able to limp in with a monster if there is already enough dead money to make him try that play. Then you get to put in a huge re-raise when it comes back around.

Bankroll requirements and profit[3]

At the beginning of the chapter, I said that the no-limit hold'em sit-and-go might be more profitable than limit cash games, on a "per risk" basis. That is, if you have a fixed bankroll, you might be able to make more money playing the sit-and-go.

This is a fairly radical statement; let's have a look at it.

Mason Malmuth has made the well-known suggestion that if you're going to play limit hold'em seriously, you should have 300 big bets in a separate bankroll (from which you're not paying rent, groceries, etc.). Another common rule of thumb is that a good player can win about one big bet per hour. Since Internet games play 2-3 times faster than brick and mortar ones, let's assume that our good limit hold'em player can win two and a half big bets per hour. So, a "good" player in a $5-10 limit cash hold'em game might be able to win $25/hour. Not bad. Based on Malmuth's criterion, he would need a bankroll of 300 x $10 ($3000) to be relatively safe from ruin.

---

[3]There is a chapter "Bankroll Considerations" beginning on page 236.

Now, suppose you took that same $3000 and invested in sit-and-go play. Jim Geary, a highly respected poker professional,[4] estimates that a good player needs about 25 buy-ins to be relatively risk-free of ruin. A player with an expected (average) win of 0.33 buy-ins per event and a standard deviation of 2.0 buy-ins per event would require a bankroll of 28 buy-ins to achieve a 1% risk of ruin.[5] I am persuaded by the results of players I know that a "pretty good" player can achieve these expected and standard deviation numbers in all but the highest buy-in events, especially if you play as snugly as I recommend.

If you need 28 buy-ins, then a $3000 bankroll would allow you to play $107 buy-in events (3000 divided by 28 is about 107). This is a convenient number since most sites charge a $9 fee for a $100 sit-and-go ($109 total), and the $107 is close enough to that for our purposes.

Now, how much can you average playing $100 sit-and-go tournaments? As I said above, I think that 1/3 of a buy-in per event is sustainable. So a "good" $100 sit-and-go player should be able to make about $30-35/event. But a sit-and-go doesn't last an hour; the average is nearer 45-50 minutes. And of course, the longer your average time in a sit-and-go, the more money you're making (you're coming closer to participating in the last hand of the event). So let's take $33/event, call it an average of 50 minutes per event, add 10 more minutes (20%) to get an hourly rate, and you're at $40/hour — 60% more than our limit cash game hero!

Note also that if you are focused enough to play two games at once, you can increase that hourly income rate without increasing your bankroll requirements. You won't double it (playing two games will cost you some expectation at each), but it will

---

[4]Jim is also an internationally ranked Scrabble player.

[5]For the math-savvy reader, the expression for your required bankroll is $-(S^2/(2 \times E)) \times \ln(R)$ where (S^2) is your standard deviation per event, squared; E is your expected win per event; ln(R) is the natural logarithm of your desired probability of ruin. For further discussion of this, consult any good probability and statistics book.

still increase markedly. This is, of course, true for the cash player as well, but it further spreads the absolute dollar earning potential between the two.

Of course, there are many variables to this equation. A player who is a "good" limit cash game player may simply not have the temperament for committing all his chips on a single hand. Other players take advantage of weakness in no-limit games by routinely moving most or all of their stack into the middle. These people are often stunningly unsuccessful at limit poker because their bullying tactics aren't as effective when they can only bet a small percentage of the pot.

So a good player in one form of the game might be a fish in another. When deciding which form(s) to play, you must look inward (and at your results) to see where your strengths and weaknesses are.

An afterthought on no-limit hold'em

Interestingly enough, no-limit hold'em has much stronger Darwinian properties than its limit cousin; good players beat bad players more efficiently and decisively. I believe that limit poker has contributed to the huge growth of the game in American casinos and cardrooms. And conversely, the Europeans' unwillingness to play anything but no-limit and pot-limit poker has cost the continent dearly in terms of poker's popularity.

After all, if a poor player has no chance against a good player, then he rapidly tires of getting beaten and losing his money. Limit poker is a great equalizer — because you are often making calls with relatively large pot odds, even "bad" calls are not mathematically terrible. But when a player is calling half of his chips for a gutshot draw, or invests his whole stack in top pair when his opponent has him out-kicked, he is taking *far* the worst of it. A finite bankroll simply won't tolerate that sort of abuse. Of course, even in limit poker, the good players will eventually take the money from the bad players. But it can be a slow process so dominated by variance that the losers don't feel the pain so acutely. So they keep coming back for more, remembering the wins and conveniently forgetting the greater losses.

The media have told us that no-limit hold'em is the Cadillac of poker games, and for now, people seem to believe that. But though I am hesitant to predict things of this nature, I think there will be a limit (as it were) to how long this fascination with no-limit hold'em will last. The "generous" player will eventually migrate to a game where his bankroll lasts longer.

With that said, I see no reason to pass up sit-and-go tournaments (and their profits), even though I have concerns about their ultimate effect on poker, and am suspect of their longevity. As a worker in the poker industry, I can worry about those things. As an author, I would be remiss in not discussing the profit opportunities that the sit-and-go provides.

Quiz on the No-Limit Hold'em Sit-and-Go

Questions 1-6 apply to the following situation: it is the first round of blinds (blinds are 10-20) in a one-table no-limit hold'em sit-and-go. You and the other players each have about 1500 chips. You are in middle position, halfway between the blinds and the button.

1. It is folded to you in middle position, and you have KK. How much would you raise? Now, suppose you have AQ instead. How much would you raise?

2. Two players have called in front of you. How much would you raise with KK? How much with AQ?

3. It's folded to a player who raises to 60 chips. Do you call or re-raise with KK? If you re-raise, how much? And answer the same questions for AQ and KQs.

4. You are the first one into the pot, and raise to 60 chips. It's folded to the player on the button, who makes it 200. What would you do with QQ? What would you do with AK?

5. A player has jammed pre-flop four of the last six hands and won the pot all four times. One time he was called by a player with TT. He had 98 and made two pair, so now he has 3100 chips. He jams all-in again. Which of these hands would you call with: KK, AK, 55, 76s?

6.   Three players call the 20 chip big blind in front of you. Which of these hands would you call with: 44, T9o, 54s, A8s?

Questions 7-14 apply to the following situation: you have 1400 chips and the blinds are 10-20. You get A♥-K♣ and raise to 80 chips after one caller. There is one caller behind you, and the original caller calls as well. There are now 270 chips in the pot.

7.   The flop comes T♠-5♠-3♥ and the first player checks to you. What would you do?

8.   The flop is the same T♠-5♠-3♥, and the first player to act on the flop bets 180 chips. What would you do?

9.   The flop comes T♠-5♠-3♥, and the first player to act on the flop bets 30 chips. What would you do?

10.   The flop comes A♠-T♠-3♥ and the first player checks. What would you do?

11.   The flop comes A♠-T♠-3♥, and the first player bets 180. What would you do?

12.   The flop comes A♠-T♠-3♥, and the first player bets 30. What would you do?

13.   The flop comes A♠-T♠-3♥ and the first player checks. You bet 200 chips and just the first player calls. The turn is the 9♣. The first player checks. What would you do?

14.   The flop comes A♠-9♠-3♥, and the first player checks. You bet 190 chips and just the first player calls. The turn is the J♣. The first player checks, you bet 480 chips, and he check-raises all-in for 800 more. You have 700 chips remaining. What would you do?

Questions 15-16 apply to the following situation: you are down to 1300 of your original 1500 chips. You are the fifth chip stack of six remaining players. The blinds are 100-200.

15. Two people have folded in front of you. What would be your action with each of the following hands: AJs, JTs, 88, 44?

16. The third highest chip stack has raised to 600 in front of you. What would you do with each of the following hands: AJs, JTs, 88, 44?

Questions 17-18 apply to the following situation: the blinds are now 100-200, but you have increased your chips to 3400, and are the second chip leader. There are six players left. The third chip leader has 2500 chips.

17. It is folded to you in the cutoff position. The big blind is in fourth chip position with 1600 chips after posting his blind. What would you do with each of the following hands: AJo, A8s, 44, QTs?

18. The short stack player goes all-in for 700 chips and it's folded to you on the button. What would you do with the following hands: KK, 99, AQ, A4, 55?

Questions 19-21 apply to the following situation: there are four players left, three places pay. The blinds are 100-200. You have 800 of your original 1500 chips left, and are in fourth place.

19. You are first to act. What would you do with each of the following hands: A3o, 66, 98s, KQ?

20. You post your big blind of 200 chips (leaving you 600). The chip leader, acting first, raises to 1000 chips. It's folded to you. What would you do with each of the following hands: A2s, QJs, 66, 76s?

21. You post your big blind of 200 chips, and get 77. The chip leader, acting first, raises to 400 chips. It is folded to you. What would you do?

Questions 22-23 apply to the following situation: there are four players left, three places pay. The blinds are 200-400. You are the chip leader with 6000 chips.

22. You are first to act. The second chip leader is on the big blind with 3600 chips after posting his blind. What would you do with each of the following hands: ATo, A4s, 77, QJo?

23. It is folded to you on the small blind. The big blind is the third chip stack with 2500 chips (including his blind). The short stack, who will get the big blind next, has 1000 chips. What would you do with each of the following hands: ATo, A4s, 77, QJo?

Questions 24-25 apply to the following situation: you are down to two players. You are approximately even in chips: you have 7000; your opponent has 6500. The blinds are 1000-2000 with a 100 chip ante.

24. You are the button (and thus the small blind). What would you do with each of the following hands: QQ, K5o, 33, QJo?

25. You are the big blind, and now have 5900 chips after posting the ante and big blind. Your opponent raises all-in. With which of these hands would you call: A2s, 44, T9s, KTo?

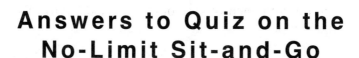

Answers to Quiz on the No-Limit Sit-and-Go

1. A good rule of thumb is to raise to *three times the big blind* if you're the first one in. So in this case, you'd raise to 60 chips. You should make that raise with *any* hand you're going to raise, simply to avoid giving patterns in your raises.

2. Add the two callers to your standard "three times" raise, and so make the raise about five times the big blind — 100 chips total.

3. Any "big" hand with which you'd normally raise, you should re-raise. A good-sized raise would be how much you could raise in a pot limit game. With 30 chips in blinds, and a raise to 60 chips, your (theoretical) call adds another 60 chips, so you could raise 150 more (to 210). Raising to 200 would be just fine. You should fold KQs and similar hands as they could easily be dominated by the original raiser's hand. You could *call* with pocket pairs since you're getting the right price to flop a set (7% of the amount you can win is about 100 chips; you only have to call 60).

4. With QQ (and KK and AA), you would re-raise to about 700 or 800, and plan to put the rest of your chips in on the flop. If an overcard to your big pair came on the flop, it's a difficult situation. With AK, AQ, JJ, and TT, you should call the re-raise, and look at the flop. If you flop top pair or better, move in. If not, be prepared to fold.

5.   You should call with AA-QQ or perhaps JJ. Other than that, you should not get involved, not even with AK. There is no reason to risk your entire stack this early in the event on what may be a close decision.

6.   You can call with 44 if you don't fear a raise behind you. Call with A8s if you can be relatively sure of seeing the flop without a raise *and* your opponents are likely to give free or cheap cards on the flop.

7.   A good bet in this situation is *2/3 - 3/4 of the pot*. So 200 would be a good bet. Note that you're (semi-) bluffing here. You really want to win the pot on the flop. It's a close decision to bet at all because there are two callers. If there are more than two callers, don't bet.

8.   Fold. He may have just a spade draw, but that's the way it goes. He made an honest bet and you have to give up here.

9.   This is more difficult; your opponent has made a "tester" bet. Either he doesn't particularly like his hand or he's trying to sucker you in. Generally, it means he's weak. You have two reasonable choices: (1) raise and hope to take the pot away from him right there, (2) fold. You can't call because you only have four outs that you really like, and they don't give you the nuts. Raise or fold depending on what you've observed about this player and his small bets. If you're not sure, fold.

10.   The same bet as you'd make with a ten-high flop, but this time you really do think you have the best hand. 200 chips would be a good bet.

11.   Raise. A "pot" raise would be 630 chips to 810. So raising to 800 would be great. At this point, you're pot-committed and will have to call a re-raise or jam.

12.   Raise. You need to scale your raise somewhat to his feeler bet, but also pay attention to the current pot size. A "pot"

raise would be 330 chips to 360. Raising to 350 would be fine.

13. You were supposed to have the best hand on the flop, and you're still supposed to have the best hand. There are 670 chips in the pot; a good bet would be 450.

14. If his player notes say something about being extremely tight or never check-raising with less than two pair, then folding is correct. Otherwise, you need to call all-in, although you're not thrilled about it. If the flop had been A♠-T♠-3♥, then hands like KQ and JT are now beating you. Fold in this situation.

15. Both AJs and 88 are worth a raise. If you raise to 600 chips and are called, there will be 1200 chips in the pot and you'll only have 700 chips left, which is too close to leaving you pot-committed. So you should just move all-in before the flop with both of those hands. With huge hands (AA-QQ), you might consider putting in the standard raise (hoping to attract a call) and then moving the rest of the chips in on the flop. In this case, don't even look at the flop; just move in. With JTs or 44, you don't have enough chips to play speculative hands and they're not strong enough to raise. So fold.

16. AJs and 88 are near the lower end of what you'd be willing to re-raise all-in. So it's close between jamming and folding. If the raiser is likely to be weak, tend to jam. If he is capable of raising and then folding, tend to jam. If you have a good chance of sneaking into the money (because of the table dynamics), tend to fold. Fold JTs and 44.

17. Note that you can put in a standard raise without going below the current third place chip stack. And the big blind should be giving up a lot of hands. So you can raise with *all* of these hands. But fold A3o without hesitation.

18. With 99 or AQ, you'd like to isolate the short stack and make it a heads-up contest. So you should jam to discour-

age either of the blinds from playing. With KK, you *might* consider just calling and see if you can trap somebody for a call. If you do, move in immediately on any ace-less flop. Fold A4 and 55.

19. The blinds are about take away 300 of your 800 chips, leaving you in desperate straits. Jam with any ace, any king, any pair. Jam with the 98s only if the big blind is likely to fold.

20. You need to take a stand here — the A2, QJ, and 66 are enough to do it. You can fold kings with small kickers, but call with any pocket pair.

21. This is a perfect situation for the stop-and-go play. Call the raise and then shove your remaining chips in on the flop without regard to what it is. If you're having a good day, the raiser will have AK, miss the flop, and fold to your jam.

22. With your big chip lead, you should be beating up on the other stacks. You should put in a standard raise (to 1200 chips) with each of these hands.

23. You should jam with every one of these hands. You want the big blind to fold. You hope that he will notice the tiny stack about to be in deep trouble, and simply fold. But you want to make it clear to him that he will have to commit *all* of his chips to this hand if he wishes to play.

24. Any of these hands is worth a jam if the blinds are that high. If the blinds were lower, you might put in a standard raise and hope to win the big blind without committing all your chips. With a huge hand like QQ, you might actually *call* (if that won't get your opponent nervous) and hope that either he raises pre-flop, or gets enough of the flop to commit his chips.

25. The A2 has the danger of being dominated by any pair or any other ace. The T9s has no high-card value. You are best off folding them and calling with KT or 44.

Section IV

Miscellaneous Topics
Bibliography
Glossary
Index

Player Stereotypes

You will quickly learn that you spend a relatively small percentage of your time at the poker table actually playing a hand. The dealer spends time shuffling the cards and dealing, selling chips, etc. Furthermore, after reading much of this book, you've discovered that you don't get to play very many of the hands you're dealt. So, what do you do when you're not in a hand?

Study your opponents and the way they play.

While each player has his own playing style, there are some general categories into which most players fall. Understanding these categories will help you know how to play against different kinds of players.

Loose-passive — the "calling station"

This is one of the best kind of players to have in your game. He has learned that any two cards can win in hold'em, and he would hate to be out of the pot if his hand would have been a winner. He will call before the flop with just about any two cards. Often, he will continue calling throughout the rest of the hand until it is inescapably obvious that he can't win. Furthermore, the loose-passive player won't do much raising. Mostly, he calls. An important point: it is virtually useless to try to bluff him — he'll call no matter what hand you represent.

Now here's the *really* good news: a large percentage of the players you play against in low-limit hold'em games will be loose-passive. They will occasionally catch some miracle draws to make very good hands, but over the long haul, they will steadily give away their chips.

Loose-aggressive — the "maniac"

The loose-aggressive player is much more difficult to handle. He, too, plays a lot of hands, but he likes to raise. He'll raise with any ace, or any two suited cards. If there is a re-raise behind him, he'll often say, "Cap it!"[1] with little regard for his cards. He wants to *gamble*. On later betting rounds, he'll bet and raise with anything, hoping to scare people out of the pot. He *loves* to bluff.

This kind of player will eventually lose his money, too. He plays too many hands that have no value, and bluffs in places where he has no hope of being successful. However, he will create much more confusion than the calling station, and he will win some pots through sheer bluster. When a maniac gets on a run of good (or lucky) cards, he can fill up chip racks as fast as the chip runners can bring them. A maniac can be very good for you if you have a good hand, because he will do all the betting for you. However, you will occasionally find yourself throwing away the best hand against this kind of player.

Furthermore, a maniac will greatly increase your variance.[2] He will be capping the betting pre-flop with almost random hands. A maniac or two at a table can make the pots humongous, but you'll have to risk a lot of chips to win one of them.

Tight-passive — the "rock"

This sort of player is perhaps most common in Las Vegas and Reno. Often, he'll be a retiree who can't afford to be throwing a lot of money around the table. He's played a few thousand hours, and has a pretty good idea of which hands are good and which are not. The rock doesn't like speculative hands and generally avoids fancy plays — he likes to "get two big cards and

---

[1]"Cap" means to put in the last raise. If there are only three raises permitted, by putting in the third one, he "caps" the betting.

[2]"Variance" is a statistical term describing the swings you have away from your expected results. The higher the variance, the larger the up and down swings in your bankroll.

bet'em."[3] While these players are fairly predictable, you aren't likely to make a lot of money from them.

Tight-aggressive — the solid player

This is the kind of player *you* want to be. He doesn't play very many hands, but when he does, he tends to take control. He will use the check-raise to freeze up bettors or cause weaker players to make playing mistakes. He will raise for value and to get free cards. He is aware of the pot odds at all times, and makes the correct play based on them.

This kind of player is dangerous. Optimally, you'd like to be the only player of this type at your table. If you see too many of them when you sit down, you should look for another table.

Categorizing your opponents

So how do you tell what kind of opponents you're up against?

Before you get into a game, stand on the rail and watch the players. Pick two players and watch them for two full rotations of the button around the table — about 20 hands. One saw the flop 19 times, never raising, but calling all the pre-flop raises. It's a fair guess that he's a calling station. The fellow next to him played in only three pots during that time, and raised once. It's harder to tell when somebody is playing a small number of hands, but you want to be more careful of the second player — he's (probably) being more selective about the cards he plays.

In the game, watch what cards players show down. Suppose a player raises pre-flop and then shows down 95s; that doesn't mean very much. But if he raises three times in 10 minutes and shows down similar hands every time, you may start to suspect that he's got maniacal tendencies. You can also learn things by hands players *don't* show down. For instance, if a player calls a bet on the end, and then throws away his hand when shown top pair, you know he couldn't beat it. What hands could he have had? Try to figure out what kinds of cards he was playing.

---

[3]This straightforward approach to hold'em success has been attributed to poker legend Johnny Moss (although Johnny was anything but a "rock").

Of course, if you're playing online, you can use the notes feature or tracking software (which you can read about on page 167). Realize that even if you're not using such software to track your opponents' play, some of them are using that software to track yours.

Note also that players can change categories, either intentionally or unconsciously. If they're doing it intentionally, look out. A player who knowingly shifts gears in his playing is one to be respected. However, a player may go "on tilt" because he's lost too many hands, too much money, or simply gotten too many good hands beaten. Then he can turn into a maniac for a while and start calling and raising with terrible hands. Be alert for this behavior so you can take advantage of it.

Bluffing and Implicit Collusion

Bluffing is rarely correct in low-limit hold'em games.

Please go back and read that first sentence again. Now say it out loud. You may find this a surprising and disturbing statement. What is poker without bluffing? You needn't worry — there will be plenty of bluffing in your low-limit hold'em game. However, *you* should not be the one doing it. In this chapter, we will explain why.

If you get into a pot with one or two opponents, bluffing is an integral part of the game. However, in low-limit games, you rarely have one or two opponents — you have five or six or more. The probability of a bluff working against any one of them is perhaps quite high (in fact, you will normally have some of them beaten). However, the probability of your bluff working against *all* of them, which it must to succeed, is exceedingly low. We call this concept "implicit collusion." Effectively, the whole table is colluding against the bluffer (you) — *somebody* will call and catch your bluff.

In general, for a bluff to be correct, you must believe it will be successful often enough to pay for itself. Suppose all the cards are out and you have missed your flush draw. Now it's checked to you, the last player to act. There are 15 big bets in the pot. Your bluff, if it works, will win 15 bets for you. If unsuccessful (i.e., you are called), you lose one bet. So your bluff must succeed once in every 16 tries to be a break-even proposition. If it succeeds more than that, you are making money; less than that, you are losing. Against a lot of players, even 15:1 on your bluff may not be sufficient. The implicit collusion effect, especially if the pot is large, will overwhelm the value of your bluff.

When should you bluff?

Very rarely.

That said: you should do it when the pot has been limited to a very few players, but is quite large. Suppose you have

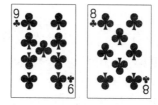

in late position. Four players call in front of you, as do you. The little blind raises, a player in the middle re-raises, you call the other two bets. Now the little blind caps the betting and everybody calls. There are 24 small bets in the pot before the dealer puts out the flop, which comes

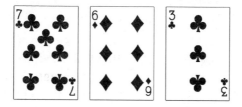

The little blind bets and gets three callers. You raise and everybody calls. That's 10 more small bets for a total of 34 bets. The turn is the 4♠. The little blind bets again, and you are the only caller. The river is the 2♦. Now the little blind checks. There are now 19 big bets in the pot — if the little blind will fold once in 20 hands like this, your bluff is worth it. However, if you suspect that the little blind actually has a *worse* hand than you (perhaps you have A♣-K♣ instead of 9♣-8♣), you should check the hand down. This is because you might run into a check-raise bluff and you can't call.

Remember, however, many players will not fold once in a *hundred* times like this. When up against such a player, save the last bet and check the hand down, even if you have no hope of winning in the showdown.

Catching a bluff

Some players seem to get a huge rush from bluffing, and will do it in spite of being caught on a regular basis. In bigger games, you might have to make a stand once in a while to catch them. However, in a low-limit game, your fellow players are acting as an ad hoc posse against this potential pot thief. You should feel no reason to participate. If you think the pot odds justify a call, do so, but don't call simply to "keep him honest."

Once in a while, you will get caught bluffing and *still win*. This is another strange phenomenon of low-limit poker. A player will decide to catch your bluff and call — but without cards strong enough to beat your bluff. When this happens, you have gained enormously. Not only have you gained the advertising value of the bluff, but you still win the pot. Because of this behavior, you should bluff with the strongest of your bad hands and missed draws.

Of course, you should *never* call if you can't beat a bluff. If you are certain your opponent is bluffing, but you can't beat a bluff, you must raise and hope that he will fold. This is a very high variance play and you must use it sparingly. It is a classic situation where the only reasonable choices are fold and raise — you cannot call.

Getting caught bluffing

On those rare occasions when you *do* try a bluff, you will occasionally get caught. Many players, for some reason, immediately throw their hands away in this situation. They are giving away the one advantage of being caught when they're bluffing — advertisement. Your opponents will remember your bluffs far better if you show them down, and then will be more inclined to call you when you have a big hand.

You might even consider announcing your hand: "There — beat that pair of fours!" It might make your opponents remember your rare bluff that much better.

A final thought on bluffing

In *Super System*, his extraordinary poker text, Doyle Brunson says the following:

> **If you're in a *loose* game, where the first man is as likely to have 7-6 as A-K, and where almost every pot is being raised, you can normally** *forget about* **putting people on hands before the Flop. You can also** *forget about* **doing anything "fancy". You're going to have to show down the best hand to win. That's all there is to it.**

Doyle is still right.

More thoughts on implicit collusion

This concept is very powerful, especially in low-limit games where you are constantly trying to outrun a lot of opponents. Another example is raising with the second best hand to limit the field to you and a single opponent. Sometimes if a player bets, you should raise even if you're fairly sure he has you beaten. Suppose he has a 40% chance to win the pot, you have a 30% chance, and the last 30% is spread out over three other opponents. Now he bets and you raise, forcing the three opponents behind you to fold. You have both benefited from this play — perhaps he has a 60% chance to win now and you have 40%. If there were originally 12 bets in the pot when he bet, you clearly should call if you have a 30% chance of winning. However, if you put in an extra bet (raise) and increase your chance of winning to 40%, you have gained more than the cost of that extra bet.

Spread-Limit Games

First let's discuss how a spread-limit game works. In a typical Las Vegas spread-limit $1-4-8-8 game, there is a big blind of $2 and a little blind of $1. It's $2 to call before the flop, but you can raise $4, making it $6 to go. On the flop, you can bet any dollar amount from $1 to $4, and $1-$8 on the last two rounds. Finally, a raise must be at least as large as any previous bet or raise on that round.

In practice, these games end up playing like structured games with a very small pre-flop bet because most players (correctly) bet the maximum on each betting round following the flop.

Buy low, sell high

This well known piece of stock market advice applies to spread-limit poker games too. When you are drawing, you would like to be calling small bets ("buying low"), but once you have the best hand, you want to charge your opponents the highest possible price to catch up with you ("selling high").

Therefore, if you think you have the best hand, bet the maximum permitted; pretend it's a structured game and that's the *only* amount you're allowed to bet. If you're drawing at a straight or a flush, you hope your opponents choose to bet less than the maximum, which they will do sometimes. For instance, an opponent may bet a small amount with top pair but a bad kicker. This is a mistake. If you believe you should bet, then you should bet the maximum, otherwise check.

Some of your opponents will continue to bet a dollar or two when they could bet as much as eight. Sadly, this sort of incorrect play has become rare, but you may see it once in a while. When an opponent gives you such a bargain, you can draw at many more hands, and when you make them, you charge your opponent full price to see the result. For instance, if there is $12 in the pot with one card to come, and your opponent bets just $1, you can call with an inside straight draw! Of course, if you do this, be sure you are drawing at the nuts, since some players will bet less than the maximum to draw you in when they have an unbeatable hand.

Since some people adjust their bet size to their perceived quality of their hand, you get wonderful information. If they bet a little, they have an "okay" hand. If they bet a lot, they have a "good" hand. If somebody is doing this, he is probably not a very experienced poker player; be careful what information you try to glean from his actions. What he thinks is a good hand and what you do might be very different.

Also, the bigger the range of permitted bets, the more drastic the difference between big pairs and drawing hands. For instance, $2-10 (on all four betting rounds) used to be a common spread-limit structure and is still found occasionally today. If you see the flop for $2, and then flop top pair, you can make it wildly incorrect for opponents to draw to straights and flushes by betting $10 on the flop. Many players did not understand the dramatic shift in value caused by this wide betting range. The result was that the bad players lost their money very quickly and the games dried up. Limits such as $1-4-8-8 have less latitude, and have pot odds situations that more closely resemble structured games.

Seeing cheap flops

The biggest change in a $1-4-8-8 game from a $4-8 or $3-6 game is that you can see many more flops because of the lower price and high implied odds. You still have to watch your position, because a $4 raise destroys the implied odds you were hoping to get by sneaking in for $2. But as you get to middle position, you can start to play almost any hand that can flop big, assuming you can do it for one bet. Any suited ace, king, queen, or jack. Any suited connector, one-gap, or two-gap. Any pair.

Pot odds

Some drawing hands that are easy calls post-flop in "structured" games (e.g., $3-$6) are not as clear in spread-limit. Since the post-flop bet may be as much as two or four times the pre-flop bet, you must think about your odds before calling with a draw.

Sometimes you can use the bet size to minimize an investment you're not altogether happy about making. Perhaps you're on the button and have flopped the nut flush draw in a $1-4-8-8 spread-limit game. Now there's a bet of $2 in front of you and one caller. You'd like to get a free card on the turn if necessary, but there aren't enough people in the pot to make a raise for value correct. Therefore, you might raise $2. This is a common enough practice (raising the bet size rather than the maximum) that it shouldn't attract too much attention. However, it may make the original bettor check on the turn.

The exception?

You might think that you could bet less when you have an unbeatable hand, hoping to get more callers. This might occasionally be correct on the river when you're trying to "sell" a very big hand. However, in general, you shouldn't do this — you're giving away information about how good your hand is, just as the novice players do when they bet good hands big and okay hands small.

Bet the maximum with your beatable *and* unbeatable hands — let your opponents guess which one you have.

Rakes and Tokes

Unfortunately, when you play poker in a public cardroom or casino, there are two taxes that you pay throughout your session: the rake and tokes.

Rakes

As we discussed before, the house makes its money in one of three ways:

1. It "rakes" an amount of money from each pot, typically 5%-10% of the pot with a maximum rake per pot.

2. It charges a fixed amount to the player who has the button each hand. That money is removed from the table, but sometimes counts as a blind bet for the player.

3. It collects a time charge, every half hour, from each player at the table.

Many players prefer the rake method — they argue that the winners are paying the house because the money comes out of the pot. If you don't win pots, you don't pay any rake.

We will discuss this idea below.

Tokes

In most public cardrooms, you are expected to tip the dealer when you win a pot. This is called a "toke" — short for "token." The typical amount varies — in Nevada cardrooms, $.50 to $1 is average. In wild and wooly California $3-$6 games, we have seen players routinely toke as much as $5 for large pots, but $1 is the normal amount.[1]

Is toking necessary? Unfortunately, dealers are paid very little (sometimes minimum wage) and earn most of their money from tokes. Thus, for the foreseeable future, toking will be a part of the game. Given that you know this, it seems rather discourteous not to toke. However, you do not have to toke $5 in a $3-$6 hold'em game. Try to toke an amount that is customary for the game in which you're playing. I personally toke better dealers more, regardless of the quality of cards they give me; I'm making my own small attempt to "pay for performance."

Tax reduction hint

As you can see, a toke is a tax on your pot. If the pot is raked (rather than time being collected on the button or every half hour), that is a further tax. If player A wins $500 in four pots, and player B wins $500 in ten pots, A pays only 40% of the tax that B does, and has a greater net win. This is yet another reason to play tight but aggressive poker — you don't want to win a lot of pots, you want to win a lot of money.

Now let's go back to the statement that raking a pot is good for the players since the winners pay the rake. You may routinely win fewer *pots* than the average player, and yet win more *money* than he does. You'll be selective about the pots you enter, and you will win a much greater percentage of those pots. Therefore, having the pot raked *is* good for you, but may not be good for the average player who makes that statement.

Play extra tight if the pot is raked

If money is removed from the pot via a rake or button charge, you must play more tightly than if you pay time on the half-hour. That's because some of the money that you collect by winning the pot is *gone*. If your game is a $2-4 or $3-6, and they're taking 5% up to $3, then (on most pots) the entire 5% is gone before you

---

[1]Note that if you play online (see "Playing hold'em on the Internet" beginning on page 163) you don't toke. For a low-limit player, this is a significant financial factor.

can get your hands on it. A fixed button charge of $3 is an even bigger bite out of your potential profit (if the pot stays under $60). So if there is money being taken from the pot, be more conservative about your starting hand requirements. Avoid the marginal hands (which isn't a bad idea anyway) and just play quality cards.

Bankroll Considerations

Many players play with too few chips in front of them.

You will occasionally hear players say that they like playing with "short stacks" (not many chips for the size of the game) because that way they can get all-in and not have to make decisions. However, poker is all about decisions. If you don't want to make decisions, don't play poker.

If you are a good poker player, you want to have plenty of chips in front of you for two reasons:[1]

1. If you make a big hand and are fortunate enough to be up against somebody who made a big (but not quite as good) hand, you want to get full value for your hand. If your opponent check-raises you on the turn with the worst hand, putting you all-in, you've missed at least two or three big bets that you should have won on that hand.

2. Not having to make a decision since you're all-in is *not* a benefit. If you are a better poker player than your opponents, your decisions are better and you can raise or fold as appropriate. If you are all-in, you are effectively reduced to calling, and can't force opponents out with check-raises, etc.

---

[1]For the curious reader, there are circumstances in which you have an advantage with a short stack. Malmuth and Sklansky have both written about this situation, but it is beyond the scope of this text. Furthermore, most players handle short stacks very poorly.

How much do you need at the table?

In a $3-$6 or $1-$4-$8-$8 game, you should start with at least $80 or $100, and have another $100 or $200 ready to put into play. In a $3-$6 structured game with a three raise maximum, it will cost you $72 (12 big bets) to cover three raises on all four betting rounds. Of course, this is an exceptional case, but sometimes you make a huge hand and have one or more people calling or raising. In that case, you want to extract maximum value. If the game is wild and there is a lot of raising, you should have the entire 12 big bets, or close to it. If the game is very tight and there's not a lot of raising, you can play with as few as seven or eight big bets.

Since the game is table stakes, you won't be permitted to go into your pocket for more money during the hand, so you must have the maximum you'd want to bet in front of you before the hand starts.

You will often see your opponents buying into the game for the minimum — perhaps $20 or $30. Each time they bust out (and they seem to do that frequently), they rebuy for that same amount. Furthermore, players who buy in this manner often want to gamble with just those few chips. They will raise or re-raise in an attempt to get all-in early in the hand, almost regardless of their cards. Be aware of this sort of behavior — in that case you can't play marginal hands or draws because you'll have to pay lots of money for them early. Play premium big cards and pairs. Note also that when a player is all-in, implied odds cease to exist. If you make a drawing hand, he has no money with which to pay you off. Therefore, when drawing against a player who is all-in, you must be getting correct pot odds right there.

Finally, you can almost *never* bluff a player off his last couple of chips. Don't bother trying.

How much do you need in your bankroll?

The answer to this question is not as simple as the one above. For instance, you may think of your bankroll as a completely separate financial entity that may be added to or removed from only at the poker table. If this is your view, then Mason Malmuth's research suggests you need about 300 big bets ($1800 for a $3-6 player) to ride out the inevitable downward swings.[2]

However, many people don't separate it out. If they have a few extra dollars, they might go play some poker. If they win, fine. If they lose, that's okay too. If that's how you prefer to manage your money, then you don't need a particular bankroll size - you simply replenish it (or withdraw from it) as you see fit.

By the way, I find the former approach (a separate bucket labeled "poker bankroll") to be an excellent disciplinary tool. Even if your financial circumstances permit you to add to the bankroll, it's healthy to monitor its growth (and shrinking), and keeping it separate will make that possible. It also attenuates the emotional swings associated with wins and losses. If you don't view a win as, "Oh boy, a new stereo!" or a loss as, "Oh dear, what of the rent?" then you'll play a better poker game all around.

I should note that I have many friends who have parlayed very small bankrolls in the $2-4 and $3-6 games into five-figure bankrolls with which they're playing serious mid-limit poker. This is not easy, and demands time, work, and a little luck. But if you start out with a reasonable bankroll for your low-limit game (so you don't go bust when you lose a few times) then you, too, can do it.

---

[2]If, of course, you're a winning player. If you're a losing player, no bankroll is big enough.

Tips for Playing in a Public Cardroom

If you've been playing poker in a home game and decide to play in a public cardroom, casino, or online, there are some rules and conventions of which you're probably not aware. Some of these are generally observed; some of them are written rules. You will find most of your fellow players in a cardroom to be friendly people, but they will be unforgiving about rules violations — and ignorance of those rules is no excuse. Learn these now and it will save you a lot of grief (and a pot or two) in the future.

- When you first sit down at the game, you may be allowed to be dealt in immediately, or you may be forced to post an amount equal to the big blind. If so, wait until the button has just passed you and then post. If you post immediately *before* the blinds get to you, you will have to play the blinds very soon — you'd rather wait until they pass. This also gives you time to relax and watch the game for a few hands before you play.

- Protect your cards at all times. Keep your hand on them or put a chip or other weight on them. Otherwise, they may be fouled if folded cards hit them or the dealer accidentally picks them up. On a related subject, don't lift them up off the table. To look at them, cover them with your hands, and raise the corners slightly so you can see them. This will take a little practice, but will eventually become second nature.

- Act in turn. It's against the rules to act before it's your turn, even if you're just going to fold. Sometimes a player in front of you will act out of turn, causing you to act out of turn. Try to keep an eye on the action so you know when it really is your turn. On a related note, if the betting has been checked to you, check as well, even if you have every intention of folding at the first opportunity. Folding prematurely gives an unfair advantage to players behind you (they know *you* won't check-raise them), and is simply bad manners.

- When it's your turn to act, act as quickly on your hand as possible. If you need a few seconds to think about it, say "Time, please." This will stop the action at you so you can decide what to do. If you don't say "Time" and people act behind you, your hand may be declared dead.

- Unlike a home game, you do *not* put your chips directly into the pot. Put them in a neat stack in front of you (whether they be antes or bets). The dealer will collect them all together when he is persuaded the pot is right. If you just toss your chips into the pot, there may be a concern that you put too few in. If so, somebody may demand that the dealer count down the pot, and people will be upset with you.

- When you raise, say so before doing anything else. Otherwise, you must get all the chips for your raise into the pot with one motion. If you do not declare your raise and make a second trip to your stack for chips, you are making a "string bet" and may be required to just call. If you declare your raise verbally, you can take all the time you want to get the raise in.

- Don't fold at the end just because somebody declares a better hand than yours. Simply turn your hand over, and verify what you have. It is also the dealer's job to determine the winner, but you should check for yourself. Don't release your hand until you've seen one better than yours.

- Get in the habit of looking at your cards once and memorizing them. This will enable you to play more smoothly and concentrate on what you're doing. Any time you look back at your cards, it should be for show.

- In a table stakes game, you don't have to fold because you can't call an entire bet. Call with the rest of your chips, and the dealer will make a side pot.[1]

- Whether in a public cardroom or online, it is inappropriate (and usually against house rules) to make comments that might influence the play of the hand. If somebody bets on the river, you may *not* say, "Wow, I guess he made the flush." At the very least, this will get you some nasty looks from the other players. At the worst, you might find yourself disqualified from a tournament.

  Another example: you are on the bubble of a sit-and-go tournament. The short-stack player goes all-in, and the chip leader is contemplating a call. You would love to see him call and bust the short stack. But if you say anything (such as "Call!"), you are violating the rules of the game and may be subjected to penalties.

- Particularly in tournaments, you may not "soft-play" other players. That is, suppose you find yourself in a tournament playing a pot against your wife (husband, brother, best friend, whomever). If you don't play against them exactly as you would any other player, you are violating not only the spirit of the game but very specific rules.

- Poker is an "every man for himself" ("every woman for herself") game. You may not make agreements with other players at the table to play differently than normal. Suppose, for example, that you're in an online sit-and-go, down to three players. One of the players has computer problems and is disconnected. You may *not* agree with the other player to simply trade your blinds back and forth while eventually busting out the third (disconnected player). That is cheating.

---

[1]See the glossary for more information about the terms "table stakes" and "side pot".

Discipline

Without discipline, you have no chance of being a winning poker player.

No matter how hard you study the material in this book, the lessons you learn will be useless if you don't apply them. While that may seem easy in the comfort of your living room, it will be a very different situation when you are at the table in a public cardroom or casino.

There will be bright lights, noise, laughter, TV, smoke, music, and every other imaginable distraction around you. If you are playing in a Las Vegas style casino, there will be the incessant ringing, clanging, and beeping of slot machines. Also in Las Vegas, attractive young ladies will be offering you free liquor on a regular basis. The players at your table will be "gambling it up" — making the craziest draws, raising for fun, and capping the betting pre-flop by implicit or explicit agreement. If you follow the guidelines in this book, you will be folding hand after hand, almost like a robot. Every once in a while, you will get to the flop, and then much of the time you'll fold there. Occasionally when you get all the way to the river, somebody will hang in with a wildly improbable draw and beat the best hand you've made all evening.

And now you must go back to the question we asked at the beginning of the book: "What is your goal?"

If you want to get in and gamble with these folks, play a lot of pots, and make some of those miracle catches, feel free to do so.

But if your goal is to *win the most money,* then you have only one choice. You play the hands that you know are good and throw away the trash. You fold AX in early position without hesitation before the flop. You stay with draws that offer you the correct odds, and dump the rest. You bet for value and rarely bluff. With time and practice, you will become a strong and dangerous poker player. You may not get much "respect" at the table — it's in very short supply at low-limit hold'em tables — but you won't care much. If they want to see your strong hand and are willing to pay for the privilege, fine.

Going on tilt

This is one of the worst things that can happen to a poker player, yet it happens to all of us. You miss what seems like the twentieth straight flush draw, followed by the only big pair you've seen all night getting beaten by a runner-runner two pair. All of a sudden, your carefully developed game plan is gone, and you're playing every hand that comes along and staying in with flaky draws.

You're on tilt.

This is a good way to lose $300 instead of the $50 you were losing already. When you sense yourself heading in this direction, get up and leave. Very few of us have the energy and brilliance to play good poker while fighting for control of our game with our emotions. Go read a book, take a walk, have a bite to eat, but don't go back into your game until you are completely relaxed and under control.

Realize that you will have more bad beats put on you than you put on other players. The very definition of a bad beat means that a player should *not* have been in the hand, and yet caught a fluke card to beat the front-runner. You will not be in this situation very often. Either you will have the best hand going in, or you will be making a correct draw. Therefore, it may seem that you take more than an equitable share of bad beats. That's true, and it's a *good* thing.

Being nice to bad players

Along those lines, here is an important piece of advice: don't berate bad players. When a bad player makes an incredible catch to beat you, you will be tempted to explain to him (if not yell at him) exactly how lucky he was, that he only had two cards in the whole deck that would win the pot for him, and how could he call your raise cold on the turn?

Remember, it is the bad player from whom you make your money. If you get him upset, he may get out of a gambling mood or, worse, leave the table. Now you can't win his money. Astonishingly enough, this ill-mannered behavior toward lucky bad players is common. Instead, you should be particularly *nice* to bad players. When somebody puts a terribly bad beat on you, swallow, try to relax, and say in the calmest voice you can manage, "Good hand."

Also, berating bad players (or anybody, for that matter) is just poor manners.

Walking away a loser

You will *not* win every session.

However, many players find it extremely difficult to walk away from the table a loser, especially if they were winning earlier in the session. David Sklansky said it best: "It's all one big session." What he meant, of course, is that there's nothing magic about a specific session between the times that you walked in and out of a card club. Your goal, we hope, is to win as much money as possible *over the long term*. If the game is good and you feel good, continue playing. If the game has turned bad, you're not playing your best, or you have a dinner date with a friend, get up and walk away without a second thought.

Of course, never put a single dollar on the table that you can't afford to lose (i.e., don't play with the rent money). You must treat the chips as tokens, and not the groceries for tomorrow. You will not be able to play your best game with money you *need* — not to mention the fact that it's just poor financial management.

Playing loose and crazy in hopes of cashing out a winner is a good first step to going on tilt.

When should I stop playing?

One of the first questions new players ask is: "When should I get up from a session?" There are two different answers, depending on whether you look at the question statistically or psychologically.

Statistically speaking, if you are playing with an edge — that is, you are a winning player — there is no optimal time to stand up and leave; every minute you sit there you are making money. This means that if you are in a good game and are playing well, you should continue playing, whether you're ahead $500 or losing $500. Note also that if you are a losing player, then there is no optimal time to *sit down* — there is no way for you to beat the game.

The psychological answer is much more complex, and varies for each person. Some of us play our best when we're winning, and poorly when we're losing. For others, it's the exact opposite. You may find that when you're winning you play your best game — this is a powerful combination. On the other hand, you may start to play looser and less carefully, eventually giving back your winnings. Dealing with losing is even more difficult. Some people tighten up and play their best when they're behind. Conversely, Mike Caro discusses the concept of "threshold of misery," a point past which you don't care how much you lose. If you're susceptible to such an effect, you must have a stop-loss limit, even though such a thing makes no statistical sense.

Folding

Early in the book, we told you that we'd teach you to win by folding. As we approach the end of this text, it's well to review some of the reasons that you should fold. So, you should be looking for a reason to fold if:

1 You look at your first two cards and *don't* think, "Hey, cool."

2. There's a raise in front of you pre-flop.

3. On the flop, you don't have top pair or better, an open-end straight draw, or four-card flush draw.

4. An unimaginative player raises on the turn and you don't have the pot odds to outdraw him if you're behind.

5. On the river, you have a marginal calling hand but there are other callers in front of you, or players to act behind you.

Of course, you shouldn't fold in *every* one of these situations, nor should you necessarily call if none of these apply. But these guidelines will help you get out of hands that are likely to cost you money.

Here's a tip about folding pre-flop: many experienced poker players will encourage you to not look at your cards until the action gets to you. This does indeed insure that you won't give away any tells to the other players before you act. However, I think that when you're new to the game, you're better off looking at your cards *immediately*. If for no other reason, it will give you time to find the reasons to fold. Often our first instinct is to put money in the pot; a little time to think may allow you to find an important reason to wait for the next hand.

The effect of all this folding

Throughout this text, we've tried to emphasize the importance of playing just good solid cards. If you follow our guidelines, you will be playing half or a third as many hands as your average opponent — maybe *fewer*. This means you won't be leaking chips away here and there in bad pots, and you will pay less pot tax.

Your opponents will probably not notice you very much because you won't be a major participant in the game. Mostly, you'll fold and watch. When you finally do come into a hand, you'll wonder how they can play with you because it must be obvious that you're starting out with better cards than they are. Don't worry — you'll get plenty of action.

When you stand up and cash out a healthy profit, they'll wonder how it happened — you didn't seem to be in many pots. No, you weren't in many pots, but you won a large percentage of the pots in which you *did* participate. This is what we mean when we say "winning by folding."

Barry Tanenbaum's "Ten Common Errors"

Poker players have a well-known rule about what to do when you first sit down at the table: "Sit for thirty minutes and look for the fish. If you don't see him, it's you." You might reasonably ask, "Okay — but how do I spot the fish?" The answer: mistakes. If you can spot mistakes that your opponents are making, then you have an edge over them in the game. If you can't spot mistakes, then either they're not making them, or you don't understand the ones they're making. In both cases, it's best to find a different game.

Barry Tanenbaum has prepared a wonderful list called "Ten Common and Costly Hold'em Errors" for the seminars and poker lessons that he gives.[1] He has graciously allowed me to reproduce that list here; it is an excellent metric of your own play and that of your opponents.

You should memorize this list.

Preflop

1.   Calling raises with inadequate values

2.   Raising in the blinds with the wrong hands

---

[1]I have attended Barry's seminars and taken lessons from him. They are always entertaining and highly educational; I highly recommend both.

On the flop

3. Improper betting from the button

4. Raising with draws when next to act after the bettor

5. Playing unimproved small pairs after the flop

On the turn

6. Not betting/raising with the best hand on the flop or turn

7. Calling raises on the turn with one pair

8. Not taking the free card when it's needed

On the river

9. Not betting the river when you're leading

10. Not betting the river when you make your hand

Conclusion

We wish we could say that now that you've read this book, you are a good or great low-limit hold'em player. Unfortunately, that's probably not true. However, we can say:

You now have the tools you need to become an excellent low-limit hold'em player.

Study, study, study

From here, you start your real education, playing as much hold'em as you can. Read this book again, and the books that we recommend in the next chapter. When a hand or a session goes badly, stop and think about what happened. Did you play poorly or did the other players get lucky? Remember, it's very easy to put the blame for bad results on others, but you should review your own play carefully first.

Begin to develop the talents you need to perfect your play at low-limit and to move up to bigger and tougher games. As we said in the introduction, there is no recipe for winning at hold'em. Learn to make the right decision most of the time. When should you raise with that gutshot straight draw and when should you throw it away? Review your mistakes and learn from them. When you got your flush beaten by a bigger one, could you have lost one fewer bet? Watch your opponents constantly. Why are they at the table? Are they happy and gambling, or are they intense, focused players like you? Are they playing on short stacks or do they have a lot of chips? Does the player in seat five know what a free card play is? The player in seat seven is having a snifter of brandy. Is that his first or fourth? How does his play change when he gets some alcohol in him? It's a lot to notice and take in, but you won't be playing many hands — you'll have *plenty* of time to watch and study your opponents.

Talk to your poker buddies. Discuss hands with them and how you might have played them differently. Learn who the good players are and watch them — you will undoubtedly pick up a few tricks (though it may cost you a few bets).

Then advance

If you want to move up to higher stakes, we encourage you to do so, once you can beat the low-limit games regularly over an extended period of time (hundreds of hours). Then be sure to read Sklansky and Malmuth's *Hold'em Poker for Advanced Players* before advancing to the bigger games.

You may be tempted to advance to a bigger game after two or three straight sessions in which you win a lot of money. Note that the swings in poker, *particularly* the wilder low-limit games, are huge and inevitable. Three straight winning sessions are not a guarantee that you're ready to move up, nor are three straight losing sessions a guarantee that you should give up the game.

Above all, maintain a positive attitude, discipline, and patience. Those are the key components of becoming a winning low-limit hold'em player.

Afterword

I can't end this book without some comment about poker and perspective.

When Chris Ferguson (2000 World Series of Poker World Champion) and I were discussing possible quotes for him to contribute to the back of the second edition, we agreed that our favorite was:

Surely you have something better to do with your time than play poker. I suggest a walk outside, volunteering at a homeless shelter, or listening to Bach.

It didn't make the back cover, but it deserved inclusion in this text.

Poker is a wonderful game and a delightful diversion. But it is not a substitute for life, and I see far too many people for whom it *is* life. Don't let yourself be one of those people.

Care for your family, friends, and neighbors. Get outside as much as possible. Tend to your spiritual needs, whatever they may be. Listen to good music. I commend to you Palestrina, the aforementioned Bach, Jerry Douglas, and Ladysmith Black Mambazo, but listen to whatever moves your soul. Read good books. I like mysteries, particularly Sharyn McCrumb and Ellis Peters. Chris Ferguson is a James Clavell fan. Be an informed citizen and use your vote.

Stay well, and thank you for reading our book.

Bibliography

The recent surge in poker's popularity has, not surprisingly, created a burgeoning market for books on the subject. The major book chains are now devoting multiple shelves to poker books, where you used to squint to find one or two lonely volumes. This review doesn't cover every good poker book (there are too many to read), but you shouldn't be disappointed by any listed here.

Alvarez, A. *The Biggest Game In Town*. Chronicle Books, 2002 (the most recent edition). This book is a true story about Las Vegas and high-limit poker players. You will not learn a thing about how to play better poker, but this is a must read for poker players. With all due respect to McManus and Holden, Alvarez is probably the best Writer to take on the subject of poker. You can smell the cigarette smoke in his prose.

Brunson, D. *Super System*. Avery Cardoza Publishing, 1979. This is the "Bible" for poker players. Some of the material is outdated because games and game structures have changed, and players have improved. That said, you cannot call yourself a serious poker player if you haven't read this book. The section on no-limit hold'em is still the standard reference on the subject.

Card Player Magazine. 3140 S. Polaris Ave. #8, Las Vegas, NV 89102 (702-871-1720). *Card Player* is a twice-monthly publication covering the poker scene around the world, as well as blackjack and sports betting. People such as Barry Tanenbaum and Bob Ciaffone are regular contributors, and I have written for them for many years.

Caro, M. *Mike Caro's Book of Tells*. Cardoza Publishing, 2003. Caro's best book. It gives volumes of information on how to read "tells" — a poker player's unintended signals about the quality of his hand. The book is much older than its publication date indicates. It was re-released by Cardoza.

Harrington, D. and Robertie, B. *Harrington on Hold'em*. 2+2 Publishing, 2004. Dan Harrington is one of the most admired (and feared) cash and tournament no-limit hold'em players in the business. This book is filled with example hands and scenarios, and Harrington's thinking is crystal clear. This is arguably the one book you should read on no-limit hold'em tournaments.

Harroch, R. and Krieger, L. *Poker For Dummies*. IDG Books, 2000. This is an excellent introductory text written in the "Dummies" books' usual breezy style with many side bars and such.

Holden, A. *Big Deal*. Abacus, 2002. This is the paperback edition; the hardback was published by Viking in 1990. This is a wonderful narrative book on poker. Anthony Holden, a well-known writer, biographer, and serious poker player in the U.K., took a year off to be a professional poker player. This is his player's eye view of medium- and high-limit games, as well as the big poker tournaments. Holden is a world-class writer, and you won't be able to put this book down. Read it after Alverez's *The Biggest Game In Town* for chronological reasons.

Krieger, L. *Hold'em Excellence*. ConJelCo, 2000. I can highly recommend Lou's book, which, unlike most, is good for beginning hold'em players. His discussion of playing AK pre-flop is particularly important.

Malmuth, M. *Gambling Theory and Other Topics*. 2+2 Publishing, 1999. Mason Malmuth is one of the top theorists in poker today (as well as being an extremely strong mid-limit player). This book is a series of essays — some about poker, some about blackjack, and some about gambling in general. Anything Mason Malmuth writes is worth reading.

Malmuth, M. *Poker Essays*. 2+2 Publishing, 1991. More essays, all of these about poker. Mason is an intense, straightforward writer, and his essays are jam-packed with good information.

McManus, J. *Positively Fifth Street*. Picador, 2004 (paperback). McManus did what Holden and Alvarez only hoped to do. He was sent to Las Vegas to cover the World Series of Poker and the trial of two people accused of murdering Ted Binion, a member of the family that owned Binion's Horseshoe, where the WSOP was held. As if he weren't busy enough, he took his expense money and parlayed it into the final table of the 2000 WSOP final event (Anthony Holden called this "the equivalent of NASA sending a poet to the moon"). This extraordinary book weaves sex, poker, politics, and the judicial system into a seamless (and seamy) whole.

Miller, E. *Small Stakes Hold'em*. 2+2 Publishing, 2004. If you are a beginner and plan to read only two books about limit hold'em, you should reread the one that you have in your hands, and then read Miller's book. His information is spot on, and the writing is a step up from the occasionally awkward 2+2 prose.

Phillips, L. *Zen and the Art of Poker*. Plume, 1999. This book is one of the few that addresses two of the biggest problems that most poker players have: ego and discipline. Most poker players are incapable of always playing their "A-game" because their emotions and ego overcome them at the table (or the keyboard). This book helps address that problem.

Sklansky, D. *Theory of Poker*. 2+2 Publishing, 1994. David Sklansky is another poker player/author who has written some of the seminal work on poker theory. This is arguably the best book on poker ever written. First published in 1987, it has become a classic in the field. It is not easy reading, and you will want to read it after you've played a lot of poker. However, to quote Sklansky himself, "If there's something I know about the game that the other person doesn't, and if he's not willing to learn or can't understand, then *I take his money*."[1] Read this book.

---

[1]This quote is taken from Alvarez's book, *The Biggest Game in Town*, listed above.

Sklansky, D. and Malmuth, M. *Hold'em Poker for Advanced Players*. 2+2 Publishing, 1999. This is one of the "Advanced" series (they also have a book on seven card stud and a book by poker expert Ray Zee on high-low split games with an eight or better qualifier). Each book is considered the current reference for its game. Do not attempt to take on medium- or high-limit hold'em games without virtually memorizing this book.

Glossary

Action   (1) Opportunity to act. If a player appears not to realize it's his turn, the dealer will say "Your action, sir." (2) Bets and raises. "If a third heart hits the board and there's a lot of action, you have to assume that somebody has made the flush."

Ante   A small portion of a bet contributed by each player to seed the pot at the beginning of a poker hand. Most hold'em games do not have an ante; they use "blinds" to get initial money into the pot.

All-In   To run out of chips while betting or calling. In table stakes games, a player may not go into his pocket for more money during a hand. If he runs out, a side pot is created in which he has no interest. However, he can still win the pot for which he had the chips. Example: "Poor Bob. He made quads against the big full house, but he was all-in on the second bet."

Backdoor   Catching both the turn and river card to make a drawing hand. For instance, suppose you have A♠-7♠. The flop comes A♦-6♣-4♠. You bet and are called. The turn is the T♠, which everybody checks, and then the river is the J♠. You've made a "backdoor" nut flush. See also "runner."

Bad Beat   To have a hand that is a large underdog beat a heavily favored hand. It is generally used to imply that the winner of the pot had no business being in the pot at all, and it was the wildest of luck that he managed to catch the one card in the deck that would win the pot. We won't give any examples; you will hear plenty of them during your poker career.

Big Blind   The larger of the two blinds typically used in a hold'em game. The big blind is a full first round bet. See also "blind" and "small blind."

Big Slick   A nickname for AK (suited or not). Its origins are unknown (to me, anyway).

Blank	A board card that doesn't seem to affect the standings in the hand. If the flop is A♠-J♦-T♠, then a turn card of 2♥ would be considered a blank. On the other hand, the 2♠ would *not* be.
Blind	A forced bet (or partial bet) put in by one or more players before any cards are dealt. Typically, blinds are put in by players immediately to the left of the button. See also "live blind."
Board	All the community cards in a hold'em game — the flop, turn, and river cards together. Example: "There wasn't a single heart on the board."
Bot	Short for "robot". In a poker context, a program that plays poker online with no (or minimal) human intervention.
Bottom Pair	A pair with the lowest card on the flop. If you have A♠-6♠, and the flop comes K♦-T♥-6♣, you have flopped bottom pair.
Brick & Mortar	A "real" casino or cardroom with a building, tables, dealers, etc. This is in contrast to an online poker site.
Bubble	(1) The point at which only one player must bust out before all others win some money. (2) The person who was unfortunate enough to finish in that position.
Burn	To discard the top card from the deck, face down. This is done between each betting round before putting out the next community card(s). It is security against any player recognizing or glimpsing the next card to be used on the board.
Button	A white acrylic disk that indicates the (nominal) dealer. Also used to refer to the player on the button. Example: "Oh, the button raised."
Buy	(1) As in "buy the pot." To bluff, hoping to "buy" the pot without being called. (2) As in "buy the button." To bet or raise, hoping to make players between you and the button fold, thus allowing you to act last on subsequent betting rounds.
Buy-In	An amount of money you pay to enter a tournament. Often expressed as two numbers, such as $100+9, meaning that it costs $109 to enter the tournament; $100 goes into the prize fund and $9 goes to the house.
Call	To put into the pot an amount of money equal to the most recent bet or raise. The term "see" (as in "I'll see that bet") is considered colloquial.
Calling Station	A weak-passive player who calls a lot, but doesn't raise or fold much. This is the kind of player you like to have in your game.

Cap	To put in the last raise permitted on a betting round. This is typically the third or fourth raise. Dealers in California are fond of saying "Capitola" or "Cappuccino."
Case	The last card of a certain rank in the deck. Example: "The flop came J-8-3; I've got pocket jacks, he's got pocket 8's, and then the case eight falls on the river, and he beats my full house."[1]
Center Pot	The first pot created during a poker hand, as opposed to one or more "side" pots created if one or more players goes all-in. Also "main pot."
Chat	Typed conversation that you can have with other players at an online poker site (or any online gathering, for that matter).
Check	(1) To not bet, with the option to call or raise later in the betting round. Equivalent to betting zero dollars. (2) Another word for chip, as in poker chip.
Check-Raise	To check and then raise when a player behind you bets. Occasionally you will hear people say this is not fair or ethical poker. Piffle. Almost all casinos permit check-raising, and it is an important poker tactic. It is particularly useful in low-limit hold'em where you need extra strength to narrow the field if you have the best hand.
Chop	An agreement between the two players with blinds to simply take their blinds back rather than playing out the hand if nobody calls or raises in front of them.
Clean Out	A card that would almost certainly make your hand best. If you are drawing at a straight, but there is a flush draw possible, then the cards that make your straight but also the flush are not clean outs.
Cold Call	To call more than one bet in a single action. For instance, suppose the first player to act after the big blind raises. Now any player acting after that must call two bets "cold." This is different from calling a single bet and then calling a subsequent raise.
Come Hand	A drawing hand (from the craps term).
Complete Hand	A hand that is defined by all five cards — a straight, flush, full house, four of a kind, or straight flush.
Connector	A hold'em starting hand in which the two cards are one apart in rank. Examples: KQs, 76.
Counterfeit	To make your hand less valuable because of board cards that duplicate it. Example: you have 87 and the flop comes 9-T-J, so you have a straight. Now an 8 comes on the turn.

---

[1]See, there's your first bad beat story.

	This has counterfeited your hand and made it almost worthless.
Crack	To beat a hand — typically a big hand. You hear this most often applied to pocket aces: "Third time tonight I've had pocket aces cracked."[2]
Cripple	As in "to cripple the deck." Meaning that you have most or all of the cards that somebody would want to have with the current board. If you have pocket kings, and the other two kings flop, you have crippled the deck.
Crying Call	A call that you make expecting to lose, but feel that you must make anyway because of the pot odds.
Cut-Off	The position (or player) who acts one before the button.
Dead Money	(1) Money contributed to a pot by a player no longer in the pot. (2) A player in a tournament who has no realistic chance of winning.
Dog	Shortened form of "underdog."
Dominated Hand	A hand that will almost always lose to a better hand that people usually play. For instance, K3 is "dominated" by KQ. With the exception of strange flops (e.g., 3-3-X, K-3-X), it will always lose to KQ.
Draw	To play a hand that is not yet good, but could become so if the right cards come. Example: "I'm not there yet — I'm drawing." Also used as a noun. Example: "I have to call because I have a good draw."
Draw Dead	Trying to make a hand that, even if made, will not win the pot. If you're drawing to make a flush, and your opponent already has a full house, you are "drawing dead." Of course, this is a bad condition to be in.
Equity	Your "rightful" share of a pot. If the pot contains $80, and you have a 50% chance of winning it, you have $40 equity in the pot. This term is somewhat fanciful since you will either win $80 or $0, but it gives you an idea of how much you can "expect" to win.
Expectation	(1) The amount you expect to gain on average if you make a certain play. For instance, suppose you put $10 into a $50 pot to draw at a hand that you will make 25% of the time, and it will win every time you make it. Three out of four times, you do not make your draw, and lose $10 each time for a total of $30. The fourth time, you will make your draw, winning $50. Your total gain over those four average hands is $50-$30 = $20, an average of $5 per hand. Thus calling the $10 has a positive expectation of $5. (2) The amount you expect to make at the poker table in a specific

---

[2]That's *two* bad-beat stories in this one chapter. See our point?

time period. Suppose in 100 hours of play, you win $527. Then your expectation is $5.27/hr. Of course, you won't make that exact amount each hour (and some hours you will lose), but it's one measure of your *anticipated* earnings.

Extra Blind A blind put in by a player just entering the game, returning to the game, or otherwise changing his position at the table. See also "blind" and "post."

Family Pot A pot in which all (or almost all) of the players call before the flop.

Fast Play To play a hand aggressively, betting and raising as much as possible. Example: "When you flop a set but there's a flush draw possible, you have to play it fast."[3]

Fish A poor player — one who gives his money away. It's a well-known (though not well-followed) rule among good players to not upset the bad players, because they'll stop having fun and perhaps leave. Thus the phrase, "Don't tap on the aquarium."

Flop The first three community cards, put out face up, all together.

Fold Equity The extra value you get from a hand when you force an opponent to fold. That is, if you don't have to see a showdown, your hand has more value than if you do.

Foul A hand that may not be played for one reason or another. A player with a foul hand may not make any claim on any portion of the pot. Example: "He ended up with three cards after the flop, so the dealer declared his hand foul."

Free Card A turn or river card on which you don't have to call a bet because of play earlier in the hand (or because of your reputation with your opponents). For instance, if you are on the button and raise when you flop a flush draw, your opponents may check to you on the turn. If you make your flush on the turn, you can bet. If you don't get it on the turn, you can check as well, seeing the river card for "free."

Free Roll One player has a shot at winning an entire pot when he is currently tied with another player. For instance, suppose you have A♣-Q♣ and your opponent has A♦-Q♥. The flop is Q♠-5♣-T♣. You are tied with your opponent right now, but are free rolling, because you can win the whole pot and

---

[3]Please don't show this phrase to any English teachers. "Play" is a verb, and thus should be modified by an adverb; "fast" is an adjective. However, if you say "Play quickly" that usually implies that time is collected every half hour, and people want you to make your playing decisions without hesitation. "Play fast" is an idiom unique to poker.

your opponent can't. If no club comes, you split the pot with him; if it does come, you win the whole thing.

Gap Hand A starting hand with cards more than one rank apart. For instance, T9 is a one-gap hand. 86 is a two-gap hand.

Gutshot Straight A straight filled "inside." If you have 9♠-8♠, the flop comes 7♣-5♥-2♦, and the turn is the 6♣, you've made your gutshot straight.

Heads-Up A pot that is being contested by only two players. Example: "It was heads-up by the turn."

Hit As in "the flop hit me," meaning the flop contains cards that help your hand. If you have AK, and the flop comes K-7-2, it hit you.

House The establishment running the game. Example: "The $2 you put on the button goes to the house."

Implied Odds Pot odds that do not exist at the moment, but may be included in your calculations because of bets you expect to win if you hit your hand. For instance, you might call with a flush draw on the turn even though the pot isn't offering you quite 4:1 odds (your chance of making the flush) because you're sure you can win a bet from your opponent on the river if you make your flush.

Jackpot A special bonus paid to the loser of a hand if he gets a very good hand beaten. In hold'em, the "loser" must typically get aces full or better beaten. In some of the large southern California card clubs, jackpots have gotten over $50,000. Of course, the jackpot is funded with money removed from the game as part of the rake.

Jam To move all-in in a no-limit (or pot-limit) game.

Kicker An unpaired card used to determine the better of two near-equivalent hands. For instance, suppose you have AK and your opponent has AQ. If the flop has an ace in it, you both have a pair of aces, but you have a king kicker. Kickers can be vitally important in hold'em.

Leak A weakness in your game that causes you to win less money than you would otherwise. Example: "She takes her pocket pairs too far; it's a leak in her game."

Limp To call. Generally the term refers to pre-flop action. For instance: "He limped in early position with 77."

Live Blind A forced bet put in by one or more players before any cards are dealt. The "live" means those players still have the option of raising when the action gets back around to them.

Live Cards that are not duplicated in an opponent's stronger hand. For example, if you have A9 and your opponent has AJ, then your ace is not "live" because making a pair of aces won't do you any good. The nine, however, is live; making a pair of nines gives you the better hand.

Maniac   A player who does a lot of hyper-aggressive raising, betting, and bluffing. A true maniac is not a good player, but is simply doing a lot of gambling. However, a player who *occasionally* acts like a maniac and confuses his opponents is quite dangerous.

Made Hand   A hand to which you're drawing, or one good enough that it doesn't need to improve.

Micro-Limit   Games so small that they couldn't be profitably dealt in a real cardroom. They exist only at online poker sites. You might arbitrarily call games $.25-.50 and smaller "micro-limit."

Muck   The pile of folded and burned cards in front of the dealer. Example: "His hand hit the muck so the dealer ruled it folded even though the guy wanted to get his cards back." Also used as a verb. Example: "He didn't have any outs so he mucked his hand."

No-Limit   A version of poker in which a player may bet any amount of chips (up to the number in front of him) whenever it is his turn to act. It is a very different game from limit poker.

Nuts   The best possible hand given the board. If the board is K♠-J♦-T♠-4♠-2♥, then A♠-X♠ is the nuts. You will occasionally hear the term applied to the best possible hand of a certain category, even though it isn't the overall nuts. For the above example, somebody with A♥-Q♣ might say they had the "nut straight."

Offsuit   A hold'em starting hand with two cards of different suits.

One-Gap   A hold'em starting hand with two cards two apart in rank. Examples: J9s, 64.

Out   A card that will make your hand win. Normally heard in the plural. Example: "Any spade will make my flush, so I have nine outs."

Outrun   To beat. Example: "Susie outran my set when her flush card hit on the river."

Overcall   To call a bet after one or more others players have already called.

Overcard   A card higher than any card on the board. For instance, if you have AQ and the flop comes J-7-3, you don't have a pair, but you have two overcards.

Overpair   A pocket pair higher than any card on the flop. If you have QQ and the flop comes J-8-3, you have an overpair.

Pat	A hand that you make on the flop. For instance, if you have two spades in your hand and the flop has three spades, then you've flopped a pat spade flush.
Pay Off	To call a bet when the bettor is representing a hand that you can't beat, but the pot is sufficiently large to justify a call anyway. Example: "He played it exactly like he made the flush, but I had top set so I paid him off."
Play the Board	To show down a hand in hold'em when your cards don't make a hand any better than is shown on the board. For instance, if you have 22, and the board is 4-4-9-9-A (no flush possible), then you must "play the board": the best possible hand you can make doesn't use any of your cards. Note that if you play the board, the best you can do is split the pot with all remaining players.
Pocket	Your unique cards that only you can see. For instance, "He had pocket sixes" (a pair of sixes), or "I had ace-king in the pocket."
Pocket Pair	A hold'em starting hand with two cards of the same rank, making a pair. Example: "I had big pocket pairs seven times in the first hour. What else can you ask for?"
Post	To put in a blind bet, generally required when you first sit down in a cardroom game. You may also be required to post a blind if you change seats at the table in a way that moves you away from the blinds. Example: a player leaves one seat at a table and takes another in such a way that he moves farther from the blinds. He is required to *post* an extra blind to receive a hand. See also "extra blind."
Pot-Committed	A state where you are essentially forced to call the rest of your stack because of the size of the pot and your remaining chips.
Pot-Limit	A version of poker in which a player may bet up to the amount of money in the pot whenever it is his turn to act. Like no-limit, this is a very different game from limit poker.
Pot Odds	The amount of money in the pot compared to the amount you must put in the pot to continue playing. For example, suppose there is $60 in the pot. Somebody bets $6, so the pot now contains $66. It costs you $6 to call, so your pot odds are 11:1. If your chance of having the best hand is at least 1 out of 12, you should call. Pot odds also apply to draws. For instance, suppose you have a draw to the nut flush with one card left to come. In this case, you are about a 4:1 underdog to make your flush. If it costs you $8 to call the bet, then there must be about $32 in the pot (including the most recent bet) to make your call correct.

Price	The pot odds you are getting for a draw or call. Example: "The pot was laying me a high enough price, so I stayed in with my gutshot straight draw."
Protect	(1) To keep your hand or a chip on your cards. This prevents them from being fouled by a discarded hand, or accidentally mucked by the dealer. (2) To invest more money in a pot so blind money that you've already put in isn't "wasted." Example: "He'll always protect his blinds, no matter how bad his cards are."
Put On	To mentally assign a hand to a player for the purposes of playing out your hand. Example: "He raised on the flop, but I put him on a draw, so I re-raised and then bet the turn."
Quads	Four of a kind.
Ragged	A flop (or board) that doesn't appear to help anybody very much. A flop that came down J♦-6♥-2♣ would look ragged.
Rainbow	A flop that contains three different suits, thus no flush can be made on the turn. Can also mean a complete five card board that has no more than two of any suit, thus no flush is possible.
Rake	An amount of money taken out of every pot by the dealer. This is the cardroom's income.
Rank	The numerical value of a card (as opposed to its suit). Example: "jack," "seven."
Rebuy	An option to buy back into a tournament after you've lost all your chips. Tournaments may offer one or more rebuys or (often) none at all.
Represent	To play as if you hold a certain hand. For instance, if you raised before the flop, and then raised again when the flop came ace high, you would be representing at least an ace with a good kicker.
Ring Game	A regular poker game as opposed to a tournament. Also referred to as a "live" game since actual money is in play instead of tournament chips.
River	The fifth and final community card, put out face up, by itself. Also known as "fifth street." Metaphors involving the river are some of poker's most treasured clichés, e.g., "He drowned in the river."
Rock	A player who plays very tight, not very creatively. He raises only with the best hands. A real rock is fairly predictable: if he raises you on the river, you can throw away just about anything but the nuts.
Runner	Typically said "runner-runner" to describe a hand that was made only by catching the correct cards on both the turn

and the river. Example: "He made a runner-runner flush to beat my trips." See also "backdoor."

Satellite   A tournament that does not award cash to its winners, but a seat (or seats) in a subsequent "target" tournament.

Scare Card   A card that may well turn the best hand into trash. If you have T♣-8♣ and the flop comes Q♦-J♦-9♠, you almost assuredly have the best hand. However, a turn card of T♦ would be very scary because it would almost guarantee that you are now beaten.

Second Pair   A pair with the second highest card on the flop. If you have A♠-T♠, and the flop comes K♦-T♥-6♣, you have flopped second pair. See "top pair."

Sell   As in "sell a hand." In a spread-limit game, this means betting less than the maximum when you have a very strong hand, hoping players will call whereas they would not have called a maximum bet.

Semi-Bluff   A powerful concept first discussed by David Sklansky. It is a bet or raise that you hope will not be called, but you have some outs if it is. A semi-bluff may be correct when betting for value is not correct, a pure bluff is not correct, but the combination of the two may be a positive expectation play. Example: you have K♠-Q♠, and the flop is T♥-5♠-J♣. If you bet now, it's a semi-bluff. You probably don't have the best hand, and you'd like to see your opponents fold immediately. Nevertheless, if you do get callers, you could still improve to the best hand.

Set   Three of a kind when you have two of the rank in your hand, and there is one on the board.

Short Stack   A number of chips that is not very many compared to the other players at the table. If you have $10 in front of you, and everybody else at the table has over $100, you are playing on a short stack.

Showdown   The point at which all players remaining in the hand turn their cards over and determine who has the best hand — i.e., after the fourth round of betting is completed. Of course, if a final bet or raise is not called, there is no showdown.

Side Pot   A pot created in which a player has no interest because he has run out of chips. Example: Al bets $6, Beth calls the $6, and Carl calls, but he has only $2 left. An $8 side pot is created that either Al or Beth can win, but not Carl. Carl, however, can still win all the money in the original or "center" pot.

Slow Play   To play a strong hand weakly so more players will stay in the pot.

Small Blind	The smaller of two blind bets typically used in a hold'em game. Normally, the small blind is one-third to two-thirds of a first round bet. See also "big blind" and "blind."
Smooth Call	To call. Smooth call often implies slow playing a strong hand. Example: "I flopped the nut flush but just smooth called when the guy in front of me bet — I didn't want to scare anybody out."
Soft-Play	To go easy on another player at the table (e.g., not betting or raising against him). Suppose you and your brother are the last two people left in a hand. On the river, you have the nuts, but he bets. If you don't raise, you are "soft-playing" him. Please note that *soft-playing is prohibited in tournaments* and can result in penalties, up to and including forfeiture of winnings.
Splash the Pot[4]	To toss chips directly into the pot rather than put them in a stack in front of you. Don't do it.
Split Pot	A pot that is shared by two or more players because they have equivalent hands.
Split Two Pair	A two pair hand in which one of each of your cards' ranks appears on the board as well. Example: you have T9, the flop is T-9-5, you have a split two pair. This is in comparison to two pair where there is a pair on the board. Example: you have T9, the flop is 9-5-5.
Spread-Limit	A betting structure in which a player may bet any amount in a range on every betting round. A typical spread-limit structure is $2-$6, where a player may bet as little as $2 or as much as $6 on every betting round.
Stop-and-Go	A play where you call (rather than re-raising) a raise, but then come out betting on the next card.
Straddle	An optional extra blind bet, typically made by the player one to the left of the big blind, equal to twice the big blind. This is effectively a raise, and forces any player who wants to play to pay two bets. Furthermore, the straddler acts last before the flop, and may "re-raise."
String Bet	A bet (more typically a raise) in which a player doesn't get all the chips required for the raise into the pot in one motion. Unless he verbally declared the raise, he can be forced to withdraw it and just call. This prevents the unethical play of putting out enough chips to call, seeing what effect that had, and then possibly raising.
Structured	Used to apply to a certain betting structure in poker games. The typical definition of a structured hold'em game is a

---

[4]This phrase is used delightfully in the John Dahl movie *Rounders*, one of the few films that accurately portrays poker action.

fixed amount for bets and raises before the flop and on the flop, and then twice that amount on the turn and river. Example: a $2-$4 structured hold'em game: bets and raises of $2 before the flop and on the flop; $4 bets and raises on the turn and river.

Suited   A hold'em starting hand in which the two cards are the same suit. Example: "I *had* to play J-3 — it was suited."

Table Stakes   A rule in a poker game meaning that a player may not go into his pocket for money during a hand. He may only invest the amount of money in front of him into the current pot. If he runs out of chips during the hand, a side pot is created in which he has no interest. All casino poker is played table stakes. The definition sometimes also includes the rule that a player may not remove chips from the table during a game. While this rule might not be referred to as "table stakes," it is enforced almost universally in public poker games.

Tell   A clue or hint that a player unknowingly gives about the strength of his hand, his next action, etc. May originally be from "telegraph" or the obvious use that he "tells" you what he's going to do before he does it.

Thin   As in "drawing thin." To be drawing to a very few outs, perhaps only one or two.

Tilt   To play wildly or recklessly. A player is said to be "on tilt" if he is not playing his best, playing too many hands, trying wild bluffs, raising with bad hands, etc.

Time   (1) A request by a player to suspend play while he decides what he's going to do. Simply, "Time, please!" If a player doesn't request time and there is a substantial amount of action behind him, the dealer may rule that the player has folded. (2) An amount of money collected either on the button or every half hour by the cardroom. This is another way for the house to make its money (see "rake").

To Go   The amount a player must call if he wishes to continue playing. Example: "The big blind was $20. Sarah raised $40 more, making it $60 to go."

Toke   A small amount of money (typically $.50 or $1.00) given to the dealer by the winner of a pot. Quite often, tokes represent the great majority of a dealer's income.

Top Pair   A pair with the highest card on the flop. If you have A♠-Q♠, and the flop comes Q♦-T♥-6♣, you have flopped top pair. See "second pair."

Top Set   The highest possible trips. Example: you have T♣-T♠, and the flop comes T♦-8♣-9♥. You have flopped top set.

Top Two   Two pair, with your two hole cards pairing the two highest cards on the board.

Top and Bottom Two pair, with your two hole cards pairing the highest and lowest cards on the board.

Trips   Three of a kind.

Turn   The fourth community card. Put out face up, by itself. Also known as "fourth street."

Under the Gun   The position of the player who acts first on a betting round. For instance, if you are one to the left of the big blind, you are under the gun before the flop.

Underdog   A person or hand not mathematically favored to win a pot. For instance, if you flop four cards to your flush, you are not quite a 2:1 underdog to make your flush by the river (that is, you will make your flush about one in three times). See also "dog."

Value   As in "bet for value." This means that you would actually like your opponents to call your bet (as opposed to a bluff). Generally it's because you have the best hand. However, it can also be a draw that, given enough callers, has a positive expectation.

Variance   A measure of the up and down swings your bankroll goes through. Variance is not necessarily a measure of how well you play. However, the higher your variance, the wider swings you'll see in your bankroll.

Wheel   A straight from ace through five.

Index

About the Author

With the surge of interest in poker, Lee Jones finally left the Silicon Valley computer world and joined the poker industry. At this writing, he is the poker room manager for PokerStars.com, a leading online poker site. His favorite part of that job is talking with and meeting PokerStars customers.

His other interests include writing, scuba diving, trout fishing, and performing music. He has been trying to master the resophonic guitar (also known as the "Dobro") for the past four years.

He and his wife, Lisa, live in San Jose. At the time of publication, their older son David is a college senior and younger son John is a high school senior. Lisa teaches voice in their home, and all four of them play music and scuba dive together.

About the Publisher

ConJelCo is a publisher based in Pittsburgh, Pennsylvania that specializes in books and software for the serious gambler.

ConJelCo periodically publishes a newsletter, *The Intelligent Gambler*, sent free to our customers. *The Intelligent Gambler* carries articles by our authors as well as other respected authors in the gambling community. In addition, it is the source of information about new ConJelCo products and special offers.

ConJelCo also sells books, software and videos from other publishers. If you'd like a free catalog or to be put on the mailing list for *The Intelligent Gambler* you can write to us at:

ConJelCo LLC
1460 Bennington Ave.
Pittsburgh, PA 15217-1139

Our phone number is 412-621-6040 (for orders in the US and Canada 800-492-9210), and our fax number is 412-621-6214.

ConJelCo is also on the Internet. You can send electronic mail to us at *orders@conjelco.com*. From the World Wide Web you can reach us at URL *http://www.conjelco.com*. On our web server you'll find a complete, annotated, ConJelCo catalog, demos of software by ConJelCo and others, and lots of other goodies for the interested gambler.